Understanding

The Lonely Man of Faith

A Commentary & Companion Guide to the Essay

By Rabbi Richard Borah

Copyright © 2013

In memory of my parents Harry & Judith Borah zt´l

Thanks and appreciation:

To my wife Andrea for her patience and support.
To my rebbeim who have given me the Torah, life's most precious gift.

"God is close to the brokenhearted; and those crushed in spirit, He saves." Psalm 34

Table of Contents

Introduction

"The Lonely Man of Faith" (LMOF) is perhaps the most personal of Rabbi Joseph B. Soloveitchik's (the "Rav's") great essays. It expresses the Rav's reflections on a unique type of loneliness. In describing the nature of this loneliness, the Rav clarifies basic "existential" problems of the human experience. The term "existential" used in this context simply means that these problems stem from the basic nature of human existence and are, therefore, common to all people at all times and in all places. The essay can be divided into the following parts:

1) A description of the human being's dual nature. Each person has two highly distinct parts making up his or her personality. One part seeks what the Rav describes as "a dignified existence" and a second part which seeks what the Rav terms "a redeemed existence." The Rav calls that part of man which strives for dignity, "Adam the first", corresponding to the Adam described in the first chapter of Genesis. That part of man seeking redemption is termed "Adam the second", corresponding to the Adam described in the second chapter of Genesis.

2) The basic conflict between Adam the first and Adam the second existing within each person, remains unresolved.
In explaining this point, the Rav expresses his understanding that life internal conflict is a basic part of all human life. The dignified man's

success brings him further from redemption and the redemptive man's success comes to him only in defeat and under the most undignified of circumstances. The Rav completely rejects the ideas of the resolution of all conflict as a goal or even as a benefit to the person. He holds that it is only through experiencing conflict that a person is refined and matures in his understanding of himself and the world. Conflict is painful, but necessary and "good for the soul".

3) The modern overemphasis of dignity and the dismissal of redemption as a human need.

In modern society, with its focus on power and mastery over the external environment, we have become accustomed to an excess of dignity and control of our surrounding. This comes at the price of ignoring man's other, more essential dimension: the redemptive persona. The Rav holds that the recognition or quest for redemption has been almost completely lost in contemporary life.

4) Finding redemption by discovering one's unique, nature.

At the point when a person discovers his uniqueness, he simultaneously achieves redemption and realizes his inability to truly communicate this singularity with anyone else. This is the particular "loneliness" that the redeemed, "lonely man of faith" experiences.

5) The Work Community and the Covenantal Community.

The Rav describes how, by participating in these two different aspects of community, the human being fulfills the needs of each of their two personas. In the work community cooperative action to achieve dignity is the goal uniting the community members, while in the Covenantal Community prayer and a commitment to the fulfillment of the covenant with God is central. Through the Covenantal Community the loneliness of the redeemed person is addressed and relieved by a community of individuals, each alone within his or her own uniqueness, but connected through the experiencing of personal redemption and a shared commitment and dedication to God who is a full participant in this community's life.

These five themes will be discussed in the following analysis.

The Structure of this Book

This present book is a commentary to be used, ideally, along with, or after, the reading, the essay "The Lonely Man of Faith". The present book can also be read as a separate, stand-alone text, to gain insight into Rabbi Soloveitchik's understanding of the human personality and modern society. The quotes and the pages cited in this book for the "Lonely Man of Faith" essay, are from the Doubleday hardcover edition (ISBN 385-42262) originally published in 1992. **R. Borah-December 2012**

Chapter 1
<u>The Dual Nature of the Human Being</u>

The Rav begins his essay by describing two forms of loneliness. The first one described is a result of being a "man of faith", explaining the essay's title, "The Lonely Man of Faith". These are <u>not</u> two separate qualities of a person —one, being a man of faith and two, being lonely. The Rav makes clear that all men of faith are lonely and the reason they are lonely is *because they have faith.* This perspective, of course, requires explanation. The Rav states on page 4:

> "...the genuine and central cause of the feeling of loneliness from which I cannot free myself is to be found in a different dimension, namely, in the experience of faith itself. I am lonely because, in my humble, inadequate way, I am a man of faith for whom to be means to believe and who substituted "credo" for "cognito" in the time honored Cartesian maxim." (LMOF p. 4)

The Rav is stating here that loneliness and faith in God ("substituting "credo" for "cognito" i.e., -living a life centered on a personal relationship with the Creator instead of the pursuit of a purely intellectual path) are inseparably linked together. This type of loneliness is not one that is bound to any place or time. Even the forefathers (Abraham, Isaac and Jacob), the Rav explains, (pg. 2) could not escape this despair. The Rav's explanation for this inherent loneliness and the details of its character will be described in some depth when we analyze the Rav's depiction of the experience of redemptive man (Adam the second). The Rav explains the reason for this inherent loneliness by describing the clarification that a redeemed individual experiences regarding his own singularity and uniqueness. This idea is at the core of the LMOF essay. In exploring the struggles of Adam the second we will attempt to clarify the nature and cause of this "existential" loneliness.

The second type of loneliness, though connected to the one just mentioned, is primarily a result of history and the times we now live in. This loneliness is related to the displaced feeling that a "man of faith" has in modern times. Living in an era when science and technology dominate the human experience, the Rav expresses the despair of a person whose core rests elsewhere- in his personal relationship with the Creator. The Rav implies that a person needs to feel that he belongs within his society and plays some meaningful role. It is not enough for a person to be alone with God. Man is a social being and part of his joy and contentment results from having a meaningful role in his society. The Rav states with simple clarity:

I could not shake off the disquieting feeling that the practical role of the man of faith within modern society is a very difficult, indeed, a paradoxical one. The purpose of this essay, then, is to define the great dilemma confronting contemporary man of faith." (pp. 7-8 LMOF).

This second dimension of loneliness for the man of faith is not inherent in the nature of faith itself. It results from the man of faith living in a society that has so marginalized the faith experience which is at the core of his personality. The Rav is describing a world that is so enamored with the power and success of science and technology, in all its many manifestations, that it views a man of faith (i.e., - someone for whom his relationship with God defines his life and personality) as being misguided at best and absurd at worst. Does the man of faith have a place in this society? The Rav states:

Let me spell out this passional experience of contemporary man of faith. He looks upon himself as a stranger in modern society, which is technically minded, self-centered, and self-loving, lost in a sickly narcissistic fashion, scoring honor upon honor, piling up victory upon victory, reaching for the distant galaxies, and seeing in the here-and-now sensible world the only manifestation of being. What can a man of faith like myself, living by a doctrine which has no technical potential, by a law which cannot be tested in the laboratory, steadfast in his loyalty to an eschatological vision whose fulfillment cannot be predicted with any degree of probability, let alone certainly, even by the most advanced mathematical calculations-what can such a man say to a functional utilitarian society which is *saeculum*-oriented and whose practical reasons of the mind have long ago supplanted the sensitive reasons of the heart?" (LMOF p. 5-6)

The Structure of the Essay and Its Difficulties

The Rav addresses the place of the man of faith in contemporary society by clarifying the basic nature of the human being's personality and, in doing this, brings to light the essential role the man of faith has in any society-even one that is so deeply immersed in the pursuit of science and technological mastery of the physical world. One of the challenges of understanding this essay is that the Rav is defining two very different elements of loneliness-one resulting from the basic nature of being human and the other from the struggle of a man of faith to find his role in a modern, technological world. This difficulty in the essay is compounded by the very distinct approaches the Rav uses to clarify these two states of loneliness. He clarifies the meaningful role of the man of faith in modern society by exploring the nature of the human personality and its dual nature consisting of Adam the first and Adam the second. It is this explanation of man's basic nature that results in an answer to the questions of:

1) Why man is inherently ("existentially") lonely? What is it about his nature that causes this phenomenon?

2) What is the essential role that the man of faith plays in this contemporary society? What is it about the nature of man that places the "faith gesture" at the core of the human experience regardless of the level of technology and mastery of the physical environment?

In defining these two core aspects of the human personality, termed "Adam the first" and "Adam the second", the Rav also clarifies the dual aspect of the human societies that result from this dual individual. The explanation of these two communities, the Work Community and the Covenantal Community, are an important part of the Rav's response to the question of what is the place of the man of faith in modern society. We will see that the man of faith, though somewhat marginal in the Work Community, is at the core of the Covenantal Community. Just as there is an Adam the first dimension and an Adam the second dimension to every individual, there is a Work Community dimension and a Covenantal Community dimension to every human society. Regarding the second loneliness of the man of faith in a technological world, the Rav clarifies that there is an essential role for Adam the second to play in providing meaning and stability to the conquests and mastery of the world that has been accomplished by Adam the first.

At this point we will begin to explore the essay more deeply by describing the Rav's explanation of the two parts of the human personality- Adam the first and Adam the second.

Chapter 2

Adam the First and the Ascent of Dignified Man

The Rav utilizes the two very distinct, descriptions of man in chapters 1 and 2 of Genesis as the Biblical expression of the dual nature of the human personality. The Rav isolates the particular differences in the two descriptions. In chapter 1 we are told:

1- Man's soul is created in the image of God, but we are not told how his body is formed.

2- Man is created along with woman as a pair.

3- Man is commanded to "fill the Earth and subdue it."

4- God is mentioned using only the name *"Elokim"*

The qualities listed above are those that the Rav attributes to "Adam the first" (dignified man) and his world. These are then compared with the qualities of "Adam the second" (redeemed man) whose description is given in chapter 2 of Genesis.

Regarding "Adam the second" the Rav points out the following references in Genesis:

1-Man is made from the dust of the ground and God gives him the breath of life.

2-Man is charged with the duty to "cultivate the garden and keep it".

3-Man is created by himself and Eve, only later, is created as his helpmate and brought to him.

4-God is mentioned using the names *"Elokim"* and the Tetragrammaton (Y'K'V'K').

The Nature of Adam the First

What is the nature of Adam the first? The central interest of Adam the first is to live, what the Rav calls, "a dignified life" -a life befitting of man's position in the world. The Rav explains that this sense of dignity is obtained by man through his achieving of "glory". What is "glory"? A man obtains "glory" when he achieves a significant degree of mastery and control over his environment. The Rav states:

Man is an honorable being. In other words, man is a dignified being and to be human means to live with dignity. However, this equation of two unknown qualities, requires further elaboration. We must be ready to answer the question: what is dignity and how can it be realized? The answer we find again in the words of the Psalmist, who addressed himself to this obvious question and who termed man not only as honorable but also a glorious being, spelling out the essence of glory in unmistakable terms: "Thou hast made him to have dominion over the works of Thy hands. Thou hast put all things under his feet." In other words, dignity was equated by the Psalmist with man's capability of dominating his environment and exercising control over it. Man acquires dignity through glory, through his *majestic* posture vis-à-vis his environment (LMOF pp. 14-15).

Man acquires this dignified life by achieving glory (i.e., mastery over nature). He moves from a "non-reflective, degradingly helpless instinctive life to an intelligent, planned and majestic one." (p.16) It is this separation from nature and the building of human civilization that is man's "glory" and the source of his dignity. It is not proper or fitting for man to be helpless and at the mercy of natural forces which are beyond his control.

The Rav explains:

Man of old who could not fight disease and succumbed in multitudes to yellow fever or any other plague with degrading helplessness could not lay claim to dignity. Only man who builds hospitals, discovers therapeutic techniques, and saves lives is blessed with dignity (LMOF p. 17).

But the mastery and control that Adam the first achieves as he builds human civilization up from raw nature to an orderly, sophisticated society is not accomplished in a moral vacuum. Man utilizes this mastery to fulfill his moral responsibilities. As the Rav states:

Dignity of man expressing itself in the awareness of being responsible and of being capable of discharging his responsibility cannot be realized as long as he has not gained majesty over his environment. For life in bondage to insensate elemental forces is a non-responsible and hence undignified affair. (pgs. 16-17)

This dignified life of Adam the first is not an instinctive, selfish lust for power and acquisition. It is a legitimate, appropriate drive through which a person fulfills his unique and exalted place in creation. God commanded man to rule over creation. Man is directed in the blessing of "be fruitful and multiply and have dominion over the Earth", that it is his nature, right and obligation to achieve this empowered life of majesty and control over his surroundings. This dominance over nature is termed "majesty", by the Rav, and it is this majestic role that gives man his dignity. The Rav quotes Psalm 8: "Thou hast made him to have dominion over the works of Thy hands. Thou hast put all things under his feet." This ruling over nature places man in his rightful place in the creation, but it is also bring with it the responsibility to fulfill God's commands. Without this majestic rule over nature, man is unable to perform his moral duties to his Creator. The Rav states:

In doing all this, Adam the first is trying to carry out the mandate entrusted to him by his Maker who, at dawn of the sixth mysterious day of creation, addressed Himself to man and summoned him to "fill the earth and subdue it." It is God who decreed that the story of Adam the first be the great saga of freedom of man-slave who gradually transforms himself into man-master (LMOF p. 19).

This close connection between dignity and responsibility is central to the understanding of Adam the first. The responsible use of power means to utilize it in a way that is not solely or centrally focused on self-aggrandizement, but instead the fulfillment of man's prescribed role in creation, as given by the Creator. The Torah is a system that clarifies, with precision, each person's responsibilities to oneself and to others. Without a sufficient degree of control over one's life, it becomes impossible to fulfill these obligations. For example, how can a person have the time and state of mind to study God's works if he or she is overwhelmed by poverty or illness? How can a person give charity if he cannot maintain himself and his family? How can a society build the institutions that provide justice and mercy for its members (schools, courts and hospitals) without the sufficient mastery over nature required to create a civilization in accordance with the laws of justice and mercy. Although many, including the Rav, have pointed out the challenges of modern technological civilization, there is no doubt that the productivity gains of our times have facilitated the fulfillment of Adam the first's quest for dignity in accordance with God's will. As the Rav states:

The brute is helpless, and therefore, not dignified. Civilized man has gained limited control of nature and has become, in certain respects, her master, and with his mastery he has attained dignity as well. His mastery has made it possible for him to act in accordance with his responsibility (LMOF p. 17).

As productivity continues to grow, along with control over disease, poverty and the basic forces of nature, the potential for dignity grows as well. It is this position of "majestic" control that renders man's life dignified. This dignified life is the basis of what distinguishes a human life from that of the beast. So the Rav states that this humanity (the living of a human life-not a beastly one) is dependent on this dignity. To obtain the human quality of "dignity" man must achieve "majesty" which is the mastery over the environment. But this majestic control over nature will not lead to dignity unless we carry out the fulfillment of our God-given responsibilities. It is only this "sanctified mastery" that will result in the fulfillment of our responsibilities to the Creator the dignity that we seek. The Rav sums up this confluence of dignity and its elements by stating it in the form of a "triple equation": **"humanity =dignity =glory-majesty"**. An explanation of this equation would be:

1) Adam the first cannot fulfill his humanity without the quality of "dignity". This defines his distinct and exalted position in relation to the rest of the creation.

2) Adam the first cannot achieve this "dignity" without accomplishing a sufficient degree of "mastery" over the rest of creation (nature). This is his technology for harnessing nature to fulfill human needs and places him in his exalted and intended role. This is termed "glory" by the Rav.

3) Once Adam the first establishes this control over nature ("glory"), he has achieved "majesty".

4) Once this "majesty" is accomplished man must use this power to fulfill his responsibilities to his Creator. This is the true fulfillment of the dignified life that Adam the first seeks.

Adam the First and the Quest for Beauty and Order

Adam the first, in his constant quest for a dignified life, strives to impose the theoretical constructs of his intellect onto nature. Whether it is engineering a city skyline or creating a body of societal laws, Adam the first is bringing order to chaos and reshaping the natural world to suit his purposes by creating a human civilization to suit his needs most efficiently. But the Rav clarifies that this quest for mastery is not only a pragmatic one. The quest for mastery of nature becomes a quest in itself, even when the outcomes have no practical value, per se. This too is part of the drive that results from the deepest core of man's nature to "fill the Earth and subdue it". As the Rav states:

While pursuing this goal, driven by an urge which he cannot but obey, Adam the first transcends the limits of the reasonable and probable and ventures into the open spaces of a boundless universe. Even this longing for vastness, no matter how adventurous and fantastic, is legitimate. Man, reaching for the distant stars is acting in harmony with his nature which was created, willed, and directed by his Maker. It is a manifestation of obedience to rather than rebellion against God. (LMOF p. 20)

The Rav provides important insight here for those who might suspect that man's boundless quest for technological mastery is contrary to the will of God. The Rav is quite clear that this quest for mastery is sanctioned by the Creator and constitutes a major motif in the human being's rightful progress towards a dignified life. It is not only the desire to create improvements in the quality of his life that drives man to discover and master the natural world. It is also to express his innate "majestic role" of mastery over his environment which has its own ends and compels man on to ever greater levels of understanding and mastery over the forces of nature.

Technology for Evil Ends

Man's history is replete with the use of technology for evil ends. The sadistic application of military developments by so many civilizations makes it clear that technological advances can be used for terrible purposes. Recent examples of this include the Nazi extermination machines and the terrorists' use of modern airplanes on 9/11. At the beginning of the Biblical account of mankind, the Tower of Babel is presented as a case where technological accomplishments were utilized for rebellion against God. The Torah states:

And they said, "Come let us build us a city, and a tower with its top in the heavens, and let us make a name for ourselves, lest we be dispersed across the whole Earth. God descended to look at the city and tower which the sons of man built, and God said, "Behold, they are one people with one language for all, and this they begin to do? And now, should it not be withheld from them all they propose to do? Come let us descend and there confuse their language, that they should not understand one another's language." (Noah, 11:5-7)

Just what precisely was the sin committed by the "Babelites"? It is not stated in the Torah, but Jewish sages attribute its leadership to Nimrod and the desire to "wage war against God". The Creator has sanctioned the quest for mastery over nature, not as a good in itself, but as a fulfillment of the human role in the creation. God commanded Adam and Eve: "be fruitful and multiply and conquer the Earth." However, this does not mean that technology cannot be utilized wrongly to strengthen a person's ability to rebel against God, and to seek greater abilities to carry out injustice towards others.

It is the "sanctioned" quest for mastery that the Rav describes as one that the scientist or the engineer carries out when he or she desires to understand how nature works in order to 1) experience the joy of understanding of nature's order and beauty 2) to utilize this mastery to fulfill his responsibilities as a human being created by God and to build a dignified and just human civilization.

Adam the First and the Aesthetic Quest for Beauty

As we have explained, Adam the first's quest for a dignified existence manifests itself through his separation from nature and mastery over his environment. This dignified life in accomplished not only in the scientist/mathematician, but equally in that of the artist/aesthete who seeks to create and appreciate beauty. What do the engineer and artist have in common? Both of these human endeavors create civilization through mastering the forces of nature and creating a unique human domain through the creation of beautiful buildings, gardens, clothes and other objects which attest to man's mastery over his world and his separation from the beasts in the fields. As the Rav states:

Adam the first is not only a creative theoretician. He is also a creative aesthete. He fashions ideas with his mind, and beauty with his heart. He enjoys both his intellectual and his aesthetic creativity and takes pride in it (LMOF p. 19).

Why does a person want to live in a house that is attractive, wear beautiful clothes and be surrounded by objects of beauty? Although the interest in beauty differs for different people, it is normal for a human being to have this desire to some degree. It would be rare and perhaps pathological for a person to take no interest in beauty and to have absolutely no concern for the attractiveness of his home or clothes. The Rav is clarifying a very important point. Namely, that the quest for mastery (technology) and the quest for beauty (aesthetics) results from the same root-the desire for a dignified life, with mastery over the environment and separation and distinction from raw nature. We will not find any civilization in the history of the world that did not have a strong aesthetic dimension. Even those early and technologically primitive (by modern standards) civilizations always had a highly developed aesthetic culture which manifested itself in their beautification of household objects, clothes, hair and buildings. A civilization may be struggling mightily against the elements of nature, but it will still find the time to decorate its bowls, create clothing that it considers beautiful and adorn its men and women with objects of beauty. The Rav states of Adam the first:

He is this worldly-minded, finitude-oriented, beauty-centered. Adam the first is always an aesthete, whether engaged in an intellectual or an ethical performance. His conscience is energized not by the idea of the good, but by that of the beautiful. His mind is questing not for the true, but for the pleasant and functional, which are rooted in the aesthetical, not the noetic-ethical sphere. (LMOF, p. 19)

The aesthetic, the Rav explains, is actually at the center of Adam the first's quest. He is not driven to understand what goodness and truth are in themselves. He seeks practical solutions that will help him achieve a pleasant and productive life. He considers the good to be those actions and habits that help to facilitate progress. He considers "truth" to be those ideas that will help bring about a pleasant, productive civilization, whether they are mathematical, scientific or aesthetic truths. For example, Adam the first may consider teamwork and cleanliness to be "good" traits because they contribute to an orderly and productive society. He may consider beauty and health also to be "good" because they too will lead to this functional, comfortable society. He may value geometry and gravity because by utilizing these constructs he can more efficiently create a life for man that is pleasant, functional and predictable. Both the aesthetic and functional progress that man makes establishes his majestic position above nature and his control of his own world and destiny. Both are reflections and a measure of man's dignified existence.

Chapter 3

Adam The Second-Loneliness and Redemption

In LMOF the Rav focuses on the differences between the accounts of man's creation in chapter 1 and chapter 2 of Genesis. Adam the first, (the Rav's term for Adam of the first chapter in Genesis) was given the blessing to "be fruitful and multiply, and fill the earth and subdue it and have dominion over the fish of the sea , over the fowl of the heaven and over the beasts, and all over the earth." He was created together with the woman, as it states: "so God created man in His own image, in the image of God created He him, male and female created He them." But with Adam the second (the Rav's term), described in the second chapter of Genesis, there is no woman mentioned as being created with man. With Adam the second, there is no blessing to be fruitful and multiply. Instead, the verse states: "And the eternal God took the man and placed him in the Garden of Eden to serve it and to keep it." Also, instead of the Adam the first's being created "in the image of God ", we find the verse states: "And the eternal God formed the man of the dust of the ground and breathed into his nostrils the breath of life and man became a living soul." A list of these differences, as the Rav describes them, are provided in the following table:

Adam the First	Adam the Second
1) Formed in the "image of God	1) Formed of dust and God breathed into him
2) Commanded to fill the earth and to subdue it	2) Commanded to cultivate the garden and to keep it
3) Man and woman are created together	3) Man created alone and Eve created later
4) God is called by name "*Elokeem*"	4) God is called by name "*H' Elokeem*"

The Rav builds on each of these differences in the description of man's creation, to show the how each of the two Adams represents a distinct part of the human personality. Each person is made up of two incongruous elements, which are not only different and distinct, but are also at odds with one another. The agenda of Adam the first interferes with the quest of Adam second, and vice versa. What emerges is a brilliant insight into the human condition and a characterization of human life as being a dual path made up of the quest of Adam the first and the opposing quest of Adam the second. We have described the path of Adam the first in the previous chapters as the pursuit of a dignified life. The path of Adam the second is completely different. He does not seek dignity. He seeks redemption. We will see that this goal is, in many respects, diametrically opposed to the path of Adam the first.

Adam the Second and the Three Questions:

Adam the first is curious and intrigued by the world around him, but that curiosity is connected to some type of utility. As reflected in his blessing to "fill the Earth and subdue it", Adam the first wants to understand the cosmos so that he can gain some degree of control over it and, in turn, over his own existence. Even though this mastery of Adam the first can sometimes take abstract forms such as mathematical formulae, scientific laws or aesthetic achievements, the underlying quest is the desire for mastery and the achieving of a dignified life acquired by having obtained greater control in shaping the world he lives in. But the quest for control, mastery, majesty or even for dignity, is not of interest to Adam the second. His desire to understand the world is not connected to any practical benefit or control, or to achieving an exalted self-image. The Rav states:

However, while the cosmos provokes Adam the first to quest for power and control, thus making him ask the functional "how" question, Adam the second responds to the call of the cosmos by engaging in a different kind of cognitive gesture. He doesn't ask a single functional question. (LMOF, p. 21)

We now step into the "deep end of the pool". What I mean is that the description of Adam the second provided in the essay "Lonely Man of Faith" is expressed poetically and indirectly, as opposed to the somewhat straightforward description given of Adam the first.

The clear description of Adam the first is possible due to the active nature of his quest. He has distinct intellectual and physical activities that he strives to accomplish in order to achieve the mastery of the environment, which is at the core of his interests. He creates mathematical formulae that clearly define for him the underlying patterns of cosmic activity and which fill him with a sense of empowerment and greatness. Utilizing the abilities of the human mind he has "cracked the code" of the universe, to some degree, and has risen above the mystery and the darkness to see with clarity, the underlying pattern. This knowledge also holds the promise of current or future technological innovation which will give him greater physical mastery over his environment and, therefore, greater control over his life. He may construct a new type of building, ship, weapon, phone or other device that incorporates this new knowledge. Knowledge for Adam the first is power, whether its manifestations remain abstract, or translates into technological innovations. Adam the first is a solver of problems. He wants things to be made clear by the power of his rational mind and his physical efforts. These are clear mental and physical activities that allow Adam the first and his quest to be described accurately and understandably.

This is not the case with Adam the second. What does he quest for? What are his goals and what activities does he involve himself in to achieve these goals? The Rav states:

He wants to know: "Why is it?", "What is it?", "Who is it?" (1) He wonders: Why did the world in its totality come into existence? (2) He asks: What is the purpose of all this? What is the message that is embedded in organic and inorganic matter, and what does the great challenge reaching me from beyond the fringes of the universe as well as from the depths of my tormented soul mean? (3) Adam the second keeps on wondering: "Who is He who trails me steadily, uninvited and unwanted, like an everlasting shadow, and vanishes into the recesses of transcendence the very instant I turn around to confront this numinous, awesome, and mysterious "He"? Who is He who fills Adam with awe and bliss, humility and a sense of greatness, concurrently? Who is he to whom Adam clings in passionate, all-consuming love and from whom he flees in mortal fear and dread?" (LMOF, p. 22)

Adam the second is involved in the search for meaning, not for mastery. Whereas Adam the first takes existence as a given and seeks to master it and gain control over it, Adam the second is fascinated with the idea of existence itself, and is puzzled by his own existence. While Adam the first is drawn to working out how the parts of the creation work and fit together to perform, Adam the second views existence as a whole, single entity that requires explanation.

The Rav is positing that a core part of the human personality is concerned with the quest to understand why we exist. Let's examine each of the Rav's three numbered statements in the previous quote. The numbering of the three indicates that each is a distinct element of Adam the second's personality. All three are united as well, and we need to explore both their differences and what all three have in common. The first question is: "Why did the world in its totality come into existence?" This most basic of questions starts from the innate sense that existence- the fact that there is an existence of time, space, matter, etc. requires an explanation and justification. Even existence is not a "given" to the mind of Adam the second. The Rav states: "Why did the world in its **totality** come into existence?" as the first question, I believe, to express the wonder, awe and curiosity about existence itself, and not about any particular aspect of that existence or even the organized structure of existence. It is "the existence of existence" that draws man's curiosity here. Existence itself must be purposeful, must be for an end beyond simply existing. An innate sense in man, draws him to this question. The Rav implies that this pondering about why there is existence is a legitimate, essential human interest and not an idle, meaningless or foolish one.

The second question is: "What is the purpose of all this? (What is the great challenge reaching me...?)". This inquiry of Adam the second is a bit more tangible. Man wants to know the reason that he (or she) exists. He has a sense that his life should fulfill some purpose and he longs to understand what this purpose is and how his purposeful life fits into this grand scheme of existence.

I believe that at the base of this curiosity and longing is the desire to know what the "good" is? While Adam the first is focused on how to accomplish things in the most efficient and effective manner, he does not really posit a moral direction towards which to utilize his power and technical prowess. Should he use his guns to conquer the weak and establish order in the world or to defend the weak against the strong that would conquer them? Should he use his technology for a life of maximum pleasure and indulgence or for one that is just, merciful and moderate? There is a moral interest that is, according to the Rav, at the core of the human soul. Here the search for meaning becomes quite personal whereas the first question about why there is an existence at all, is more abstract. Morality and an interest in the "good" is what the Rav expresses as "the great challenge reaching me from beyond the fringes of the universe as well as from the depths of my tormented soul."

The third question: "Who is He?" is the longing for a connection with the transcendent God that man senses. As the Rav states: "Who is He to whom Adam clings in passionate, all-consuming love and from whom He flees in mortal fear and dread?" This is the love and fear of God. This experience and inquiry is expressed as a very complex one which runs the full spectrum of human intellectual and emotional life. Intellectually, the Rav describes God as being intensely sensed even when one does not seek His presence – "Who is He who trails me steadily, uninvited and unwanted, like an everlasting shadow…", while at other times when one seeks Him out, He is hidden from our awareness…"and vanishes into the recesses of transcendence the very instant I turn around to confront this numinous, awesome, and mysterious 'He'?". The joy and dread that one simultaneously experiences upon sensing God are also complex and appear to be contradictory. The Rav states in describing this third question: "Who is He who fills Adam with awe and bliss, humility and a sense of greatness, concurrently? Who is he to whom Adam clings in passionate, all-consuming love and from whom he flees in mortal fear and dread?" The questions of Adam the second, unlike those of Adam the first, do not have definitive, communicable answers. They do not necessarily move Adam the second to a particular conclusion or even toward a specific course of action. Adam the first is focused on the question of "how" - how to accomplish the mastery over nature he seeks; how to fulfill the blessing/commandment of "Be fruitful and multiply and conquer it (the Earth)…".

Adam the second is not seeking any tangible benefit or utility from his quest. Adam the second is not attempting to discover "what works" but instead, his interest is in "what is meaningful and what is the good". This part of the human being wants to know whether his endeavors *are worthy*- whether they have some intrinsic value and goodness. Whereas Adam the first takes this world as a given and is focused on putting it under his control, Adam the second steps beyond the boundaries of the world, contemplating it as a whole and asking why it came into being and what the underlying purpose is for its existence. For Adam the second, this world is a "hint" that bespeaks of something transcendent, beyond this world, that determines its existence and meaning.

Adam the second seeks his Creator, the source of all good that has brought this world into existence for some purpose and has brought mankind into existence to play some role in this creation. All of Adam the second's questions lead back to a longing for the source of all existence, of all good. The quest for God by Adam the second takes a very different form from that of Adam the first. But this does not mean that Adam the second does not seek out satisfaction for his intense desire to gain insight regard the *"why, what and who"*. But Adam the second takes a different approach. As the Rav describes it, he seeks clarity in the qualitative world:

In order to answer this triple question, Adam the second does not apply the functional method invented by Adam the first. He does not create a world of his own. Instead, he wants to understand the living, "given" world into which he has been cast. Therefore, he does not mathematize phenomena or conceptualize things. He encounters the universe in all its colorfulness, splendor, and grandeur, and studies with the naiveté, awe, and admiration of the child who seeks the unusual and wonderful in very ordinary thing and event. While Adam the first is dynamic and creative, transforming sensory data into thought constructs, Adam the second is receptive and beholds the world in its original dimensions. He looks for the Image of God not in the mathematical formula of the natural relational law but in every beam of light, in every bud and blossom, in the morning breeze and the stillness of a starlit evening (LMOF, p. 23).

The "secret weapon" of Adam the first, in his quest for mastery over his world, is the use of the logical, creative mind to analyze and conceptualize a problem and arrive at some workable solution. Deduction, induction, definition and the formulation of experiments and theories are all in the domain of Adam the first, who applies them to grasp the patterns of nature's structure which can then be manipulated for man's purposes. In all fields of study this is the approach. In Talmud the "Brisker Derech" developed by the Rav's grandfather Rav Chaim Soloveitchik zt"l formulated a powerful method for understanding and solving problems in Jewish law. In science the experimental method developed by Bacon, Newton and others proved a tremendously powerful tool for solving scientific problems and with its application science has progressed more in the last 300 years than in the thousands of previous years.

All logic-based methods of inquiry are dependent on some form of dissection of a problem into parts which correspond to mental categories. This mental breaking down of the whole into its parts allows one to understand how something functions and how to potentially manipulate that functional mechanism. Whether one inquires about a the functioning of a living thing by breaking it up into its organs, tissues, cells and chemical reactions or one inquires about how to play music by breaking sound up into scales, notes, and time signatures, all these inquiries utilize an "atomizing" method to learn and master the object or action in question.

According to the Rav, Adam the second has no such methodology to utilize. He does not seem to use or need logic-based methods to explore his questions. The quest seems to be less rigorous, but also, perhaps, more difficult. For many of us the only familiar and meaningful form of inquiry is the logic-based methods of Adam the first. Everything else is either relegated to the realm of feeling (pain and pleasure) or emotions, such as joy, sorrow and the other emotional states. But the Rav, in speaking about Adam the second, validates the simple perception of the world ("he beholds the world in its original dimensions") undisturbed by logical categorization or definition, as being a valid source of knowledge and insight. He (Adam the second) seeks his answers, the Rav explains, by direct contact and experience with the world in its wholeness and beauty. How does this immediate contact with the creation bring insight? The Rav clarifies this, to some degree, by describing the intimate connection that exists between God and man. The Rav explains:

In a word, Adam the second explores not the scientific abstract universe but the irresistibly fascinating qualitative world where he establishes an intimate relation with God. The Biblical metaphor referring to God breathing life into Adam alludes to the actual preoccupation of the latter with God, to his genuine living experience of God rather than to some divine potential or endowment in Adam symbolized by *imago Dei*. Adam the second lives in close union with God. His existential "I" experience is interwoven in the awareness of communing with the Great Self whose footprints he discovers along the many tortuous paths of creation (LMOF pp. 23-24).

It seems to me that the Rav is answering here the question of how man's simple and direct observation of the world brings him any insight into these three most basic of questions. Since man is always in constant connection with God, he, on some intuitive level, possesses the answers to these questions. Man is in direct contact with the source of all existence and all goodness and it is the accessing of this connection that brings enlightenment for Adam the second. But the question remains, what is Adam the second to do to bring this connecting about? What is his task? What is the free-will act needed to move him forward in his quest for understanding these mysteries? Although the Rav does not give any direct methodology regarding this process, he does explain one key element in Adam the second's journey. This quest progresses not from victory and success, but instead from defeat and despair. It is through man's defeats and the humbling experiences of his life by which he accesses this intimate connection that he has with God. It is also through man's self-conquest and the defeat of self, as opposed to the conquest and defeat of nature and of others, that Adam the second achieves, what the Rav terms "cathartic redemptiveness".

Cathartic Redemptiveness of Adam the Second

The goal of Adam the first, as we have explained, is the dignity he derives from fulfilling his role as ruler over his world. The goal of Adam the second is different. The Rav explains:

> Adam the second sees his separateness from nature and his existential uniqueness not in dignity or majesty but in something else. There is in his opinion, another mode of existence through which man can find his own self, namely the redemptive, which is not necessarily identical with the dignified. (LMOF p. 25)

The purpose of Adam the second's quest is "cathartic redemptiveness". As Adam the first seeks dignity, Adam the second seeks "cathartic redemptiveness". The Rav describes this state:

> Cathartic redemptiveness is experienced in the privacy of one's in-depth personality, and it cuts below the relationship between the "I" and the "thou" (to use an existentialist term) and reaches into the very hidden strata of the isolated "I" who knows himself as a singular being. When objectified in personal and emotional categories, cathartic redemptiveness expresses itself in the feeling of axiological security. The individual intuits his

existence as worthwhile, legitimate, and adequate, anchored in something stable and unchangeable." (LMOF, p. 35)

The "cathartic redemptiveness" of Adam the second results from his awareness that he is a being that has a relationship with the Creator. As the Rav stated: "Adam the second lives in close union with God, His existential "I" experience is interwoven in the awareness of communing with the Great Self". At the point that a person actually experiences this communing with God and senses, it seems, not only the actual presence of God but the relationship between God and man, there is an opportunity for "cathartic redemptiveness". The "axiological security" that the Rav describes as "the individual intuits his existence as worthwhile" comes from the knowledge of this relationship with the Creator. This potential of the human being is not due to his or her personal accomplishment but from simply being a human being who is a creature that can have a relationship with the Perfect Existence. This gift cannot be taken away by circumstance or difficulties. This is what is meant by an "existential truth"- it results from the nature of one's existence, not from one's situation. This basic quality of humanity is describes by the "Rav" as "anchored in something stable and unchangeable."

Servitude and Adam the Second

The personal relationship that Adam the second has with God, is closely tied to his "role of a servant", as described by the Rav. This servitude or *"avdus"* is the fundamental quality of man's relationship with God. Adam the first is an *admirer* of God. He sees God's wondrous creation and tries to unravel the infinite wisdom within it. Adam the first tries to gain a degree of understanding and mastery. But he remains an observer. God is, for him, always in the third person "He".

Adam the second is a servant of God. His relationship with God is personal and interactive. He prays to God and requests his needs, standing humbly in prayer and in longing for God's grace. God is for him in the second person "You". Adam the second does not seek to "use" God or His creation. Instead, he only seeks to serve Him. Even his requests are those that will facilitate his role as servant. This is the *"eved* Hashem" (servant of God) of whom Moses was the pinnacle. Adam the second is the one who accepts the *"ole malchus shamyim"* (yoke of heaven). This acceptance is at core of the *Shema,* which each Jewish adult male must recite twice a day.

The nature of the relationship Adam the second has with God is one of servitude. This divine servitude is part of man's deepest persona and at the very core of his being. This is not a servitude of injustice or degradation, which often characterizes servitude to a human master. Servitude to God is where man finds his place in the universe and achieves personal redemption. Man is joined closely to God through this servitude and, as the Rav states, he acquires "axiological security" (a sense of his inherent worth as a being). This worth does not come from what he has accomplished, but simply from what he is. However, I would not portray this servitude as something purely joyful. The Adam the first part of a person is disturbed by Adam the second's servitude. Whereas Adam the first wants to surge forward from victory to victory and "strength to strength", Adam the second takes his humble place as a servant of the Creator, willing to sacrifice all personal strivings and plans to carry out this service.

Abraham is a profound example of a person who was derailed from the forward movement of his Adam the first persona. He accepted total servitude and compliance as an Adam the second personality carrying out God's command. When he took his son Isaac to the altar he was intending to kill, not only his miraculously born son, but also his plans and striving towards the fulfillment of his destiny as the father of the Jewish people. All would end with Isaac. All the strivings of his life to that point, it seemed, would vanish in that moment. This sacrifice is *avdus* (servitude) on the highest level. And it is only when Abraham humbly submitted to this service that he merited the Covenant – a binding personal relationship with the Creator. Only in servitude did the relationship come to life. This servitude and relationship to God is the core event and most meaningful activity of human life. It is more fundamental than any of the activities and accomplishments of Adam the first, regardless of the greatness of his successes. The Rav states:

Cathartic redemptiveness is experienced in the privacy of one's in-depth personality, and it cuts below the relationship between the "I" and the "thou" (to use an existential term) and reaches into the very hidden strata of the isolated "I" who knows himself as a singular being (LMOF p. 35).

Crisis, Defeat and Cathartic Redemptiveness

The Rav contrasts Adam the first's striving for conquest of his world with Adam the second's quest for control of self. He states:

Cathartic redemptiveness, in contrast to dignity, cannot be attained through man's acquisition of control of his environment, but through man's exercise of control over himself. A redeemed life is ipso facto a disciplined life. While a dignified life is attained by majestic man who courageously surges forward and confronts mute nature- a lower form of being-in a mood of defiance, redemption is achieved when humble man makes a movement of recoil, and lets himself be confronted and defeated by a Higher and Truer Being." (LMOF, p. 36)

When is cathartic redemptiveness achieved?: "... when humble man makes a movement of recoil and lets himself be confronted and defeated by a Higher and Truer Being". Why does the Rav contend that redemption is found in "the depth of crisis and failure" (LMOF p. 36)? There is no direct explanation of this in the text, but perhaps we can understand this from what the Rav has stated about the ongoing connection that exists between God and man, as explained in the description in Genesis, where God "breathed into the nostrils of man". As we quoted from the Rav, earlier:

The Biblical metaphor referring to God breathing life into Adam alludes to the actual preoccupation of the latter with God, to his genuine living experience of God rather than to some divine potential or endowment in Adam symbolized by *imago Dei*. (LMOF, pp. 23-24)

Perhaps since man possesses the *Tzelem Elokim* (image of God) that connects him continually and fundamentally with the source of all good, of all truth, Adam the second possesses the answers to his three fundamental questions of "Why", "What" and "Who", as described earlier. These answers, are, so to speak, a part of man's essence. They are not accessible to the logic-based function of man's intellect and this knowledge is, therefore, not subject to syllogism and the logical constructs of this type of inquiry. This is why the inquiries of Adam the second contemplate things as a whole and "experience them" as opposed to breaking them down for analysis. But a question remains as to why this innate, existential knowledge is only available to the humble, broken and defeated person?

The "parallel processing" going on in the soul of man finds the positive strivings and free will of Adam the first contending with the humble acceptance and service of Adam the second. Man is the subject of a myriad of involvements and distractions that confront him in his quest for success and mastery in his life. Adam the first is in constant pursuit of some form of success or another whether it is health, wealth, family, knowledge, societal/political power and the like. These constitute the focus of a normal human life. As mentioned, this is the legitimate involvement of Adam the first, in the fulfillment of his blessing/command of "be fruitful and multiply and conquer the Earth". As Adam the first surges forward in this quest for a dignified life he will not tend to focus on those aspects of his core personality which exist as a humble servant of the Creator; as a completely dependent and powerless being in the presence of a perfect God. When man is victorious and successful in his quest for dominion and conquest, Adam the first is "steering the ship" and man's psychic energies are directed outward toward solving problems and accomplishing goals in the world around him.

But when man's is defeated by circumstances or by personal shortcomings, and he is made to realize the profoundly fragile and insecure aspect of his existence- it is then that he understands the deepest core of his nature as a humble servant of God who is completely under the rule of the *Melech Elyon*, (the Master of the Universe). These times of defeat and crisis are the times when we are most capable of discovering this aspect of ourselves, of sensing our servitude to God. Instead of the quest for mastery, there is the quiet recognition of one's role as a servant of the source of all good, all truth and all real power. It is a private, personal and incommunicable experience that cannot be fully shared with another and is not subject to precise measurement or articulation.

The crisis and despair that leads to the cathartic redemptiveness of Adam the second is necessary to derail the constant forward momentum of Adam the first and to bring man's life to a halt. It is in this stillness, where man's understanding of himself as a passive, humble servant in the presence of God, comes to the fore. Man finds himself, at that moment, helpless and dependent on his Creator and, only in that situation, does he realizes the deep, inherent connection that exists between him and God. Out of this despair can emerge a unique sense of worth and well-being which is unattainable by Adam the first, regardless of his achievements and the dignity he acquires. As the Rav states:

When objectified in personal and emotional categories, cathartic redemptiveness expresses itself in the feeling of axiological security. The individual intuits his existence is worthwhile, legitimate, and adequate, anchored in something stable and unchangeable. (LMOF, p. 35)

This feeling of worthiness and adequacy has its own unique stability as it does not result from any success or accomplishment that the person has achieved. It results from one's realization that he exists as a fortunate being that has a connection with God. It is this existential truth that is at the source of Adam the second's sense of worthiness. This factor does not depend on achieving success through mastery of the outside world. Adam the second realizes man has been created with his most precious qualities already "built-in".

Mastery Over Oneself To Attain Cathartic Redemptiveness

It is not through crisis alone that Adam the second achieves redemption. In addition, Adam he must accomplish a different type of conquest from that of Adam the first. The Rav states:

Cathartic redemptiveness, in contrast to dignity, cannot be attained through man's acquisition of control of his environment, but through man's exercise of control over himself. A redeemed life is ipso facto a disciplined life. "
(LMOF, p. 35)

What is the connection between control over oneself and the achievement of cathartic redemtptiveness? We can speculate here based on the Rav's essay. First, it seems reasonable to assume that a person not in control of his desires and emotions would be unable to possess the state of mind necessary to sense this deeper aspect of self. Overwhelmed continually by desires and fears, a person will be constantly and desperately searching for external changes to achieve success. The person who has achieved a mastery over himself develops, along with it, a calm and reflective mind which is more capable of "being" without pursuing. It seems that this is an essential quality for achieving cathartic redemptiveness. As he Rav states:

To be" is not to be equated with "to work and produce goods" (as historical materialism wants us to believe). "To be" is not identical with "to think" (as the classical tradition of philosophical rationalism throughout the ages, culminating in Descartes and later in Kant, tried to convince us). "To be" does not exhaust itself either in suffering (as Schopenhauer preached) or in enjoying the world of sense (in accordance with ethical hedonism). "To be" is a unique in-depth experience of which only Adam the second is aware, and it is unrelated to any function or performance. (LMOF, p .40)

So we can propose that this self-mastery is needed to achieve the settled, balanced state of mind and the reflective nature necessary "to be" and to cease continual doing or planning. This state of "being" does seem to have an almost meditative aspect to it. "To be" seems to just "be" oneself without any other activity. The ability to "defeat oneself" is required in order to achieve the experience of cessation of the building, conquering and striving of Adam the first. The structure of mourning (*avelut*), exemplifies Adam the second's quality of defeat and acceptance. The mourner accepts his loss and defeat by God. The Rav's position is that in man's accepting his ultimate powerlessness and defeat (which becomes most apparent in with the contemplation of mortality), the person reveals new paths for personally relating to God in addition to those which are solely pragmatic (requesting our needs) or appreciative (praise and thanks). God, the true reality, becomes the focus and core of the person's love, longing and the focus of his intellectual and emotional life.

I would propose that there is an even more fundamental reason that self-mastery and self-control are prerequisites for the state of cathartic redemptiveness. Perhaps what is spoken of by the Rav as self-control and self-mastery is the person's free-will act of self-subjugation to the kingship of God. This act of self-limitation and service is not done out of fear or to obtain some end. God is recognized as the Creator/Maintainer of all existence and the source of all truth and goodness. Man's role is to serve the truly real Being.

A person recognizes that he or she is privileged to be the recipient of this opportunity and, through the covenant and the commandments, provided with a "paved path" and way of life that connects him or her directly to God. This joyful servitude and subjugation does not diminish or degrade a person but, on the contrary, redeems him and gives him his greatest, most exalted characteristic - that of being recognized and having a relationship with God. For the Jew, this subjugation and self-limitation takes the form of observing Jewish law. But for any person, these self-restrictions in the areas of pleasure and acquisition are necessary to adhere to the call of justice and mercy. They are necessary in all cases to bring one to the state of cathartic redemptiveness. (According to Jewish law, all peoples of the world are bound by the limitations of the seven Noachide laws, so for all people there is covenant and structure of life provided by the Creator in this process of self-subjugation to God's will.) The Rav describes this process:

Dignity is acquired by man whenever he triumphs over nature. Man finds redemption whenever he is overpowered by the Creator of nature. Dignity is discovered at the summit of success; redemption in the depth of crisis and failure..."Out of the depths have I called three, O God". The Bible has stated explicitly that Adam the second was formed from the dust of the ground because the knowledge of the humble origin of man is an integral part of Adam's "I" experience. Adam the second has never forgotten that he is just a handful of dust. (LMOF p. 36)

Avdus: The Essence of Man's Relationship To God

Why does man's personal relationship with God only begin when a person submits himself to the role of an *"eved Hashem"* (a servant of God)? Is this connection just an existential reality? Are we just made that way - "made to serve"? Perhaps we can clarify the essential aspect of this need for servitude in exploring man's exalted sense of himself. Could it be that as long as man does not embrace the role of servant, man views himself as a master? This is not necessarily in a distorted narcissistic manner. We have discussed that there is a condoned, even "blessed" life of dignity and an exalted position enjoyed by Adam the first. But when man is absorbed in this act of seeking dignity and dominion, it seems he cannot truly recognize God. He cannot "stand before God". This is not possible because the moment he does, man recognizes that, as the Rambam has stated, he (man) is a "small, dark creature…" (The Rambam describing the love of God in his text, the Mishneh Torah). Man's sense of dignity, position and dominion disappear in a moment. It is only by embracing the persona of the servant of God, the slave of God, which allows man's soul can draw close to the Creator. We resist the servitude relationship towards God, in order to preserve our dignity. We must remove the impediment caused by the maintenance of our dignity in order to engage God in a relationship. *Avdus* (servitude) requires the cessation of the process and momentum of this seeking of victory which defines Adam the first. *Avdus* occurs when man ceases from this process of dignity-seeking and serves God's will with all his heart and with all his soul. Ironically, the Rav informs us, that this cessation of seeking value in our own accomplishments is the way to open the door to the cathartic redemption experience which gives us a richer, more fundamental sense of our worth (axiological security) which results from our status as a being that is recognized and personally relates to God. This relationship is one of servitude. It is our status as a servant, sanctioned and recognized by God, which gives us a true sense of self-worth. This is the source of redemption.

The Experience of Loneliness and the Discovery of Self

Although the Rav does not articulate the details of Adam the second's discovery of his incommunicative, unique self, as a part of the cathartic redemptiveness process, we can speculate as to how it comes about. Each person is a unique human being. This uniqueness that each individual possesses is not due to his or her particular combination of human traits and accomplishments. It is not simply that all people possess the same traits in different degrees and proportions- this would bring about a different quality in each person, but would not create essentially unique individuals. What the Rav is describing is a unique essence imparted by God within each person. Each soul is an essentially a unique creation whose core does not resemble that of his or her fellow. It is, I would suggest, part of the miracle of the creation of each human being, that each is endowed by God with a soul that does not have an essence that is the same as any other human being. Perhaps it is this unique core which has some effect on the organizing of the traits and thoughts of a person. It is difficult to fathom that each human being has a unique essence, as we usually assess a person by his or her thoughts and actions and in that realm we all do share the same qualities with variations and to different degrees. It is these thoughts and activities that allow for our identification with one another and a sense that we can be understood and can understand others, to some extent. But when we are speaking of the core "being" of a person, the Rav explains, that there is no meaningful overlap. As the Rav states:

And defeated must Adam the second feel the very instant he scores his greatest success; the discovery of his humanity, his "I" identity. The "I" awareness which he attains as the result of his untiring search for a redeemed, secure existence brings its own antithesis to the fore; the awareness of his exclusiveness and ontological incompatibility with any other being. (LMOF, p. 37)

Cathartic redemptiveness, and the accompanying loneliness of the man of faith, occurs when a person awakens to the completely unique nature of his or her self. Each person's uniqueness is not accidental. It does not stem from the particular details of the individual's genetics or experiential history. It seems that this individuality is a result of being created by God with a unique soul. This uniqueness is an intentional one designed by God in each person's creation. Each of us is truly the only one of our kind in the world. Each of us has an incommunicable uniqueness to our essence.

Upon recognizing this existential individuality, a person also becomes aware of his or her worth to God and, simultaneously, his state of existential loneliness. (Existential is used here to mean a quality that results from the nature of something's existence and not due to its particular situation. Something that is existential is unavoidable and unalterable). Each human being serves God in a unique manner. The Rav goes on to describes a "double" loneliness. One loneliness occurs upon a person's realizing that his relationships which have been driven by the needs of one's Adam the first's tasks are totally inadequate for sharing the essential uniqueness he possesses, as they do not penetrate below the surface. The Rav states:

Adam the second suddenly finds out that he is alone, that he has alienated himself from the world of the brute and the instinctual mechanical state of, outward existence, while he has failed to ally himself with the intelligent, purposive inward beings who inhabit the new world into which he has entered. Each great redemptive step forward in man's quest for humanity entails the ever-growing tragic awareness of his aloneness and only-ness and consequently of his loneliness and insecurity. (LMOF, p. 37)

This is a difficult passage to understand as it seems to portray Adam the first as inhabiting the world of "the brute and the instinctual mechanical state of outward existence". This does not conform with what the Rav has stated up to this point about the legitimacy and appropriateness of Adam the first's quest for dignity in fulfillment of God's directive: "Be fruitful and multiply and have dominion…" It is true that the quest for dignity of Adam the first channels the more "brutish" elements of human nature such as aggression and sexuality in his quest for dominance and conquest. Although Adam the first utilizing a cunning and clever intelligence and is bounded by his obedience to God directives, perhaps it is Adam the first's close collaboration with the instinctual parts of his nature that the Rav describes as seeming "brutish and mechanical" in comparison to the redeemed perspective of Adam the second.

This first type of loneliness, though it may be painful and shocking, seems to have some remedy. The Rav writes that this new Adam the second has "failed to ally himself with the intelligent, purposive inward beings that inhabit the new world into which he has entered." The clear implication here, which in confirmed in later chapters of the essay, is that Adam the second has the option of entering into a new type of relationship with other "redeemed people" and now has the opportunity to join the Covenantal Community of which they are a part. So this first loneliness has a partial remedy. Adam the second has the option of joining with others who have achieved this understanding of their uniqueness. But there is a second part of this loneliness which, although it can be addressed, can never be removed. This is the existential type of loneliness which results from the realization of one's essential uniqueness and the incommunicability of one's inner self. This loneliness Adam the second cannot escape, even in the presence of others who are redeemed. Adam the second, in realizing his essential individuality, knows that he will never be able to communicate this essence to any other person. The Rav writes:

This story belongs exclusively to Adam the second, it is his and only his, and it would make no sense if disclosed to others.....By the time *homo absconditus* manages to deliver the message, the personal and intimate content of the latter is already recast in the lingual matrix, which standardizes the unique and universalizes the individual. (LMOF, p. 67)

Adam the second, like Adam the first, seeks his fulfillment by connecting with others in his community. The Rav goes on to describe two distinct types of communities corresponding to these two dimensions of Adam. Adam the first and his comrades join together in the Work Community. Adam the second finds his place with other redeemed souls in the Covenantal Community. We will now explore these two communities, each with its own distinct qualities, purposes and accomplishments.

Chapter 4

The Work Community

Just as there are these two "Adams" within each human being – Adam the first and Adam the second - so too there are two distinct types of human communities corresponding to them. The community that involves the cooperative endeavors of Adam the first with others of his kind, the Rav calls the Work Community. The community that results from the joining of Adam the second with others of his type he calls the Covenantal Community. And just as the two individual types-Adam the first and Adam the second, are polar opposites that co-exist within the same individual, so too the two types of communities, the Work Community and the Covenantal Community, also co-exist to create a single human community that embodies both elements. We will now describe the nature of each of these two communities and how each reflects the qualities, goals and interests of the type of Adam that comprises each one.

The Work Community of Adam the First

The Rav describes the motivation of Adam the first in forming a community and what he and his comrades see as the community's purpose and goal:

Adam the first is challenged by a hostile environment and hence summoned to perform many tasks which he alone cannot master. Consequently, he is impelled to take joint action. Helpless individuals, cognizant of the difficulties they encounter when they act separately, congregate, make arrangements, enter into treaties of mutual assistance, sign contracts, form partnerships, etc. The natural community is born of a feeling of individual helplessness. Whenever Adam the first wants to work, to produce, and to succeed in his undertakings, he must unite with others. (LMOF pp. 29-30)

As we would expect, the community of Adam the first is formed along pragmatic lines. People acting as a group, whether it is a small group raising a family, or a larger group forming a tribe or a nation, do so for the purpose of improving the abilities to accomplish pragmatic outcomes. In a coordinated group people are stronger, safer and more productive than when they act separately. If one gets sick, others can take care of him. If there is an attack by an enemy, the group can defend itself more effectively. If there is a fire or a flood, the concerted efforts of the group can improve the chances of survival and rebuilding. The Rav continues his description of the pragmatic advantages of the Work Community over laboring alone:

Distribution of labor, the coordinated efforts of the many, the accumulated experiences of the multitude, the cooperative spirit of countless individuals, raise man above the primitive level of a natural existence and grant him limited dominion over his environment. What we call civilization is the sum total of a community effort through the millennia. Thus, the natural community fashioned by Adam the first is a Work Community, committed to the successful production, distribution, and consumption of goods, materials as well as cultural. (LMOF p. 32)

Adam the first, by joining with others of his type, can accomplish the objective of creating a dignified life. The building of civilization is the quest and the accomplishment of Adam the first working together with his comrades. All of the technology, culture, science, health, legal systems and social structures that make up a nation, are the fruits of this Work Community. No longer subjugated by the force of nature to living like the beast of the field, the Work Community raises Adam the first up to his rightful place as master of the natural world, living in an environment he has fashioned according to his physical, social, psychological and cultural needs.

This description of the Work Community of Adam the first, at first glance, seems to be a complete one. What is really left for Adam the second's Covenantal Community to add? We will now explore those things that are lacking in Adam the first's Work Community. In many ways, the Rav implies that what is lacking in the Work Community makes up the most essential and meaningful dimension of human life and the human communal experience.

Limitations of the Work Community of Adam the First

The Rav stresses the inherent limitations of Adam the first's Work Community. The activities of this community do not address or improve the essential nature of the person. They simply improve the quality of his or her lifestyle. He is safer, better fed, more secure and pleased with his attainments. But the Rav does not equate this attainment of dignity with an improvement of the core personality. The Rav also points out the limitations of the relationship that exists between Adam and Eve in the Work Community. It is a practical, yet superficial relationship. The Rav states:

> The natural community of Adam the first enhances man's chances for successful survival, yet does not elevate or enhance his existential experience, since the latter is in no need of redemption or catharsis. Adam the first feels safer and more comfortable in the company of Eve in a practical, not ontological, way. He will never admit that he cannot, ontologically, see himself without Eve. They, Adam and Eve, act together, work together, pursue common objectives together; yet they do not exist together. (LMOF pp. 32-33)

"The Work Community" and all it entails in improving the quality of life, does not affect the in-depth personality of the person. In all dimensions of our life where we are pursuing a lifestyle improvement, the issues of our relationships are simply practical. If a person assists us in achieving our ends, they are a fitting companion. We can have companions who assist us at work or recreation (business partners or tennis partners), companions who assist us in obtaining pleasure and building a family (a husband or wife) or ones that work with us to achieve broader community ends (members of an organization, synagogue, or committee working together to build a museum, hospital or park). In all these cases, the relationship is based on the "work", in one form or another, which the group works together to achieve. You may have an intense attachment to this person or group if they help you achieve something of great value to you. You may sense that you even love a particular work companion very much. But, the Rav's points out, your love or attachment is actually to the ends that this person can help you achieve for yourself. It is a selfish love to achieve ends, and is not due to a recognition and appreciation of the other's inner, unique character and value. The Rav describes the limitations of the Adam the first relationship and describes a deeper, richer one that is possible only to the members of a Covenantal Community:

Ontologically they (Adam the first and Eve the first) do not belong to each other; each is provided with an "I" awareness and knows nothing of the "We" awareness. Of course, they communicate with each other. But the communication lines are open between two surface personalities engaged in work, dedicated to success, and speaking in clichés and stereotypes, and not between two souls bound together in indissoluble relation, each one speaking in unique *logoi*. The in-depth personalities do not communicate, let alone commune, with each other. God said unto them 'be fruitful and multiply and replenish the earth and subdue it and have dominion over the fish of the sea, and over the fowl of the air, and over everything that creepeth over the earth.' Male and female were summoned by their creator to act in unison in order to act successfully. Yet they were not charged with the task of existing in unison, in order to cleanse, redeem, and hallow their existence. (LMOF, p. 33)

The Rav will describe this "we awareness" and true in-depth companionship in his description of the members of the Covenantal Community of Adam the second, but its being mentioned here gives us a clear understanding of the boundaries and limitations of Adam the first in his Work Community. As Adam the firsts and Eve the firsts, our friends and companions suit our purposes and we gladly attempt to suit their purposes to maintain this very useful partnership. But I don't think the Rav would call this a truly fulfilling relationship, which is required to address the deeper, inner needs of the soul. For this we will turn now to a discussion of the Covenantal Community of Adam the second.

Chapter 5
The Covenantal Community

The resolution of the plight of the lonely man of faith is attained by joining of the Covenantal Community. Although this joining does not remove the loneliness that Adam the second experiences when he realizes his uniqueness, it does provide solace as he joins with other lonely people who share his condition, and in a unified effort, fulfill their deepest commitment to God and one another.

His quest is for a new kind of fellowship which one finds in the existential community. There, not only hands are joined, but experiences as well; there, one hears not only the rhythmic sound of the production line, but also the rhythmic beat of hearts starved for existential companionship and all-embracing sympathy and experiencing the grandeur of the faith commitment; there one lonely soul finds another soul tormented by loneliness and solitude yet unqualifiedly committed. **(LMOF pp. 41-42))**

The Covenantal Community's members are not joined together by some practical activity or goal that they seek to accomplish. They form a community out of a shared commitment by each individual's dedication to fulfilling the Covenant with God and to assist one another in this pursuit. They are kindred souls in that each of them has come to the realization that this Covenant, which constitutes the expression of each person's commitment to and connection with God, is the essence of his or her being and the basis for fellowship between them. Although each person expresses this Covenantal relationship in his or her own unique way, they are all joined by their recognition of this expression as being the core of their humanity. In this way they understand, sympathize and identify with each other in a manner that is not possible for the members of the Adam the first Work Community. An essential element in the Covenantal Community that distinguishes it from the Adam the first Work Community, is the presence of God as a member of the community.

The Participation of God in the Covenantal Community

While Adam the first believes in the Creator and admires His works, the Work Community of Adam the first is one of joining one person to another to accomplish specific goals. Building cities, scientific investigations, maintaining social order and economic plenty in society are its tasks. God is not an active participant in these activities. This is not the case with the Covenantal Community. Here, God is not only the inspiration for the community, but an active Partner and Participant whose presence makes possible the unique human relationships that take place within it.

The second is a community of commitments born in distress and defeat and comprises three participants: "I, thou, and He," the He in whom all being is rooted and in whom everything finds its rehabilitation and consequently, redemption. Adam the first met the female all by himself, while Adam the second was introduced to Eve by God, who summoned Adam to join Eve in an existential community molded by sacrificial action and suffering and who Himself became a partner in this community. God is never outside the

Covenantal Community. He joins man and shares in his covenantal existence. Finitude and infinity, temporality and eternity, creature and creator become involved in the same community. They bind themselves together and participate in a unitive existence." (LMOF, p. 44)

God is recognized as the source and Creator of the Adam the first Work Community. But He is not a member of that community. But here, God is the intermediary between the members of the Covenantal Community. Presented as the facilitator of the relationship between Adam and Eve, God's presence in the community is that which allows there to be this unique type of relationship between and among the human inhabitants. This requires some understanding. What is God's role that makes this type of human relationship possible and what is the nature of this Covenantal relationship between people?

Before we can explore the role of God in the Covenantal Community, we should further clarify what the Rav means by this type of community. We have said that it is composed of those individuals who have experienced some degree on the cathartic redemptiveness, which the Rav describes as at the core of Adam the second's strivings. But what is the particular structure of the community these individuals comprise? At the center of this community is the Covenant itself. What is this Covenant and why is it so central to this community? The Rav states:

61

The element of togetherness of God and man is indispensable for the Covenantal Community, for the very validity of the covenant rests upon the juridic-Halakhic principle of free negotiations, mutual assumption of duties, and full recognition of the equal rights of both parties concerned with the covenant. Both parties entering a covenantal relationship surrendered by mutual consent. The paradoxical experience of freedom, reciprocity, and "equality" in one's personal confrontation with God is basic for the understanding of the covenantal faith community. We meet God in the Covenantal Community as a comrade and fellow member. Of course, even within the framework of the community, God appears as the leader, teacher and shepherd. Yet the leader is an integral part of the community, the teacher is inseparable from his pupils, and the shepherd never leaves the flock. They all belong to one group. The covenant draws man into the society of men of faith. (LMOF pp. 44-45)

This description of the Rav certainly requires reflection and interpretation. It is interesting that although the cathartic redemptive experience comes to man when he is broken and defeated, the community that springs from the cathartic redemptive experience represents a particularly exalted aspect of human life, that is quite different from the dignified one of Adam the first and his Work Community comrades. As we stated previously, the soul of Adam the second is not focused on the mastery of his environment or the unraveling of its mysteries and conundrums in order to gain greater control over his world. Adam the second is attracted to and engaged in the close existential connection that exists between himself and his Creator. He is sensing and experiencing God's continual, ongoing contact with man, which the Rav interprets as the meaning of Genesis's description of God 'breathing into man's nostrils". This ongoing connection is the source of Adam the second's consciousness and the essence of his being. But how does the Covenantal Community emerge from this experience?

The Covenant and the Cathartic Redemptive Experience of Adam the Second

The Covenant (i.e., the revealed law and its directives) transforms the Adam the second's experience in a number of ways. First, this Covenant, with its specific requirements, solidifies and gives form to this cathartic redemptive experience, defining it and transforming it into thought and action that can comprise the activities of an individual's and a community's day to day life. Secondly, the Covenant, the Rav explains, transforms the servitude and "*avdus*" of Adam the second's relationship to one that has an element of "equality" (strange to say) between God and man.

Of course this does not mean to say that man and God share any equal qualities- this would be contrary to the most fundamental aspects of Jewish law and human reason. But, just as the President of the United States and a poor, homeless, drunkard, who both enter into a contract, are equally bound by the elements of the contract, regardless of their unequal status and qualities, so too, (so to speak) when God and man entered into the covenantal contract, whether with Abraham or with Jewish people at Mount Sinai, both God and the Jews were bound by the terms of the contract. It was not the simple imposition of the strong upon the weak, the ruler over the subjects. There was a contract made freely by both parties and it was this entering into the contract that resulted in our obligation to carry out the commandments of the Torah. The obligation to fulfill the laws is not, it seems, due the fact that God is the Creator and Maintainer of our lives and all existence! The Rav states:

The giving of the law on Mount Sinai was a result of free negotiations between Moses and the people who consented to submit themselves to the Divine Will. (LMOF p. 45)

This "freedom" is somewhat tempered. The Rav cites discussions from the Talmud explaining that there were elements of coercion that occurred in the acceptance of the Torah. However, he explains that this was in terms of the acceptance of each particular law, once they were known. However the initial comprehensive acceptance of the Torah was done freely.

It appears that God required two commitments on his part of the community: a general one to abide by the will of God while the community was still unaware of the nature of the commitment and a specific one concerning each individual law. The second commitment was assumed under constraint. (LMOF p. 46)

Why were these coercive elements introduced? The Rav explains:

> **The reason for introducing an element of coercion into the great Sinai covenant, in contradistinction, *prima facie*, to the Biblical story, lies in the idea that covenantal man feels overpowered and defeated by God even when he appears to be a free agent of his own will. (footnote in LMOF p. 46)**

So it seems that, although there are elements of servitude and of being overpowered by God within the Covenantal Community experience, (similar to the overpowered experience of an individual cathartic redemptiveness experience), there is still a basic core quality of free will in that man *chooses* to be a servant of God. Why is freedom of choice, which defines the entering into the covenant, so key to the communal experience of these redeemed individuals?

The Rav does not directly explain why the free choice decision to enter into the covenantal is essential for the formation of Adam the second's Covenantal Community. Why is this superior to a completely coercive master-servant experience which seems to be at the core Adam the second's cathartic redemptiveness? But since community is at the core the covenantal experience, we can speculate about the relationship of the Covenant to the formation of this community. We can reasonably conclude that the relationship between a willing subject and his or her king is fundamentally different from that of one who had this servitude imposed upon him. With a covenant freely entered into, there emerges the unique capacity for man to join together with God and man in a community of mutual love and recognition of each other. God becomes a community member, not only the community's Creator and king.

Definitions of the term "community" vary but often include as fundamental to it a "common interest" among the members of the community. With the Covenant, where the two parties are God and the Jewish people, both parties share a common interest in the fulfillment of the Covenant and both are bound together by being bound by the obligations of the Covenant and its fulfillment.

God's role as teacher, leader and master is dedicated to the fulfillment of this Covenant and the Jewish people as students, subjects, worshipper and adherents are similarly dedicated to the fulfillment of the Covenant. Though not equals in their roles, of course, God and the Jewish people are equally bound to the obligations each has taken on by entering into the Covenant. Without the Covenant, a servant and a master have no community of shared interests. The master possess all rights and the agenda is all his; The non-covenantal servant is coerced by fear, pain or punishment to fulfill obligations. He may share a situation or an activity with the master, but they do not both participate in community. So we can see the centrality of the Covenant in bringing God into the community, in that it transforms the experience from one of being overpowered by the Master, to one of being a willing and loving servant working together with the Master towards agreed upon ends. This working together is accomplished as man fulfills his obligations through obedience to the law and as God provides man with the optimum situation of dwelling in a situation where he has peace, plenty and the understanding of how to live a fulfilling life. This is the communal relationship between God and man. We will see that this communal participation of God also makes possible the deeper relationships between people within the Covenantal Community, just as it makes possible the personal relationship with God for each of its members.

The essential nature of the Covenant to the relationship between man and his Creator is, I believe, expressed in the structure of prayer. The *Shemoneh Esrei* in the Jewish morning and evening prayers is always immediately preceded by the recitation of the *Shema*. In this structure we can clearly see that our personal communing with God (the *Shemoneh Esrei*) requires as its prerequisite the acceptance of the Covenant, which is the essence of the *Shema* (*"kabbalos ole malchos shamayim"* - the acceptance of the yoke of heaven). So each day we renew our free will acceptance of the Covenant, and with that renewal we are able to continue to stand in the presence of, and have a close personal relationship with, God.

Chapter 6

Prayer and Prophecy: A Dialogue Between God and Man

The Covenantal Community is a prayer community. To explain the central aspect of prayer in this community the Rav explains that prayer is in the same category as prophecy, as both are acts by which a direct communication between God and man takes place. In prophecy, God speaks to man and man listens. In prayer, man speaks to God and God (so to speak) listens. The Rav states:

With the sound of the divine voice addressing man by his name, be it Abraham, Moses, or Samuel, God, whom man has sought along the endless trails of the universe, is discovered suddenly as being close to and intimate with man, standing just opposite or beside him. At this meeting-initiated by God - of God and man, the covenantal-prophetic community is established. When man addresses himself to God, calling Him in the informal tones of "Thou", the same miracle happens again: God joins man and at this meeting, initiated by man, a new Covenantal Community is born- the prayer community. (LMOF p. 54)

Prayer and prophecy are the two ways of intimate contact between God and man. These are the two activities that exemplify the constant closeness and connection of God and man expressed in the ongoing "breathing of life into the nostrils of man" (Genesis, Chapter 2) which the Rav described earlier. In both cases (the prophet and the one who prays), an individual stands in the presence of God and interacts with Him in a personal manner, either by being given specific visions and directives (the prophet) or by making personal petitions and giving praise and thanks to God (the praying person). This is not the abstract appreciation of God's perfection, which is carried out by Adam the first. Instead, these are the activities of an ongoing relationship – one that is individualized and personal.

The Rav points out that prayer and prophecy are similar in many ways. One important aspect which they both possess is the communal dimension. Prophecy is not an act that takes place exclusively between God and the prophet. In prophecy, the community is the third party. Prophecies were not given simply for the enlightenment of the prophet so that he could personally understand esoteric and deep truths. Prophecy was given to prepare him for his task of moving the members of the community to repentance. In prayer as well, we do not have a relationship that is limited to God and the individual. The petitions of the individual's *Shemoneh Esrei* prayers are always stated for the community, whether it be for health, knowledge, rescue from enemies or sustenance. The Rav states regarding prophecy and prayer:

Both the prophetic and the prayerful communities are threefold structures, consisting of all three grammatical personae - I, thou and He. The prophet in whom God confides and to whom He entrusts His eternal word must always remember that he is the representative of the many anonymous "they" for whom the message is earmarked. No man, however great and noble, is worthy of God's word if he fancies that the word is his private property and not to be shared by others. (LMOF pp. 58-59)

Regarding prayer the Rav states:

The prayerful community must not, likewise, remain a twofold affair: a transient "I" addressing himself to the eternal "He." The inclusion of others is indispensable. Man should avoid praying for himself alone. The plural form of prayer is of central Halakhic significance. When disaster strikes, one must not be immersed completely in his own passional destiny, thinking exclusively of himself, being concerned only with himself, and petitioning God merely for himself. The foundation of efficacious and noble prayer is human solidarity and sympathy or the covenantal awareness of existential togetherness, of sharing and experiencing the travail and suffering of those for whom majestic Adam the first has no concern. (LMOF pp. 59-60)

The Covenantal Community consists of the "I, the thou, and the He." Without the "He" (God), it seems, there is no possibility for true human companionship. But why is this so?

The Impact of Sin on Man's Relationship with God

The Rav makes clear that the deep personal connection man has with his Creator is bestowed upon him from his inception. As the Rav explained earlier, the second chapter of Genesis' description of God breathing life into Adam "alludes to the actual preoccupation of the later with God - to his living experience of God". So it seems that this innate awareness of God is given as a gift to man and not acquired by him through his efforts. However, the connection is disturbed, distorted, diminished, and destroyed through sin and ignorance. In describing man's most personal act of connecting to God (prayer), the Rav states:

Who is qualified to engage God in the prayer colloquy? Clearly, the person who is ready to cleanse himself of imperfection and evil. Any kind of injustice, corruption, cruelty, or the like desecrates the very essence of the prayer adventure, since it encases man in an ugly little world into which God in unwilling to enter. If man craves to meet God in prayer, then he must purge himself of all that separates him from God. God hearkens to prayer if it rises from a heart contrite over a muddled and faulty life and from a resolute mind ready to redeem this life. (LMOF pp. 65)

So the opportunity to experience this deep inner connection to God is contingent on the person's unqualified commitment to the fulfillment of the covenant and to live a just and merciful life. Only through this life path will the person be capable of standing in the presence of God. Only through this commitment will God give man the permission to stand before Him, to commune with Him and to be His personal companion. As we explained earlier, this idea is reflected in the laws of *Kriyas Shema* (reading the *Shema*) and *Tefillah* (prayer). As the Rav explains:

The Halakhic requirement of *Smichat Geh-oolah Luh-tephillah* (that the recitation of *Shema* with its benedictions be joined to the recital of *Tefillah,* the "Eighteen Benedictions,") is indicative of this idea. One has no right to appear before the Almighty without accepting previously all the covenantal commitments implied in the three sections of *Shema*. (p. 75)

The voluntary re-acceptance of the covenant, twice a day, is done in the recitation of the *Shema*. This entry into the covenant and the commitment to the service of God above all other considerations, allows man to then enter the presence of the Creator in prayer as an individual who is heard, considered and responded to by the Creator of the universe. The obedience to God's revealed agenda is not simply a following of orders, but a means of living out the innate relationship that exists between God and man. But it seems only when the priority of this relationship is put before all other considerations, does it "come to life" in the awareness of the individual as the profound experience that the Rav terms "cathartic redemptiveness". This is, in part perhaps, what the Rav means when he says that the participants in the covenant have an "unqualified commitment" to it. There is nothing that comes before it. One is reminded of the ultimate test of Abraham when he was required to offer Yitzchak to God. This was truly an act of unqualified commitment as it required him to put the service of God above all his most precious concerns. It was an exemplary act of expressing the primacy of man's commitment to the relationship he has with his Creator.

The Necessity of God's Presence in the Community to Create Meaningful Human Relationship

The presence of God within the Covenantal Community is a necessity for a deeper relationship to exist between people. This unique relationship requires a form of communication than that is impossible for Adam the first to have with his comrades in the Work Community. Describing the limitations of the Adam the first's communication the Rav states:

In the natural community which knows no prayer, majestic Adam can offer only his accomplishments, not himself. There is certainly even within the framework of the natural community, as the existentialists are wont to say, a dialogue between the "I" and the "thou". However this dialogue may only gratify the necessity for communication which urges Adam the first to relate himself to others, since communication for him means information about the surface activity of practical man. (LMOF, p. 66)

Adam the first certainly communicates with his fellows in the Work Community. But this communication is always directed towards the accomplishment of a goal. The goal can be intellectual, technological, cultural, pleasure-related or of an emotional nature. There can be a communication of information, plans, feelings and thoughts. It becomes somewhat challenging to precisely define what is missing from this community and this relationship. The Rav states regarding Adam the first's dialogues:

Such a dialogue certainly cannot quench the burning thirst for communication in depth of Adam the second, who always remains a *homo absconditus* if the majestic logoi of Adam the first should serve as the only medium of expression. What really can this dialogue reveal of the numinous in-depth personality? Nothing! Yes, words are spoken, but these words reflect not the unique and intimate, but the universal and public in man. (LMOF, pp. 66-67)

All that can be expressed in the dialogue of Adam the first is what one person has in common with another. This is how words and language function. I speak a word or phrase about something and you "understand" it to the extent it expresses something in common with your experience. But one person is simply not able to communicate the unique nature of his or her experience or self. This is the hidden person- the *homo absonditus*. As the Rav states:

Distress and bliss, joys and frustrations are incommunicable within the framework of the natural dialogue consisting of common words. By the time *homo absconditus* manages to deliver the message, the personal and intimate content of the latter is already recast in the lingual matrix, which standardizes the unique and universalizes the individual. (LMOF, p. 67)

So, there is a desire and a need human beings have to express and share this unique, deeper individual self- the deeper personal aspects of "distress, bliss, joys and frustrations" as we experience them, each in our own individual manner. But this is not possible because of the standardization of language. There is a word "joy" for example. I might say, "When my first child was born it brought me great joy." But my joy has a unique dimension as a result of my history, my nature and the particular way I perceive and conceive of the event.

No one experiences this joy as I do. All another person can understand from my communication is the aspect of my joy that overlaps in some way with the listener's experience and concept of joy. The other person cannot understand me and my unique experience. This inherent inaccuracy is not usually a problem with surface, work activities. For example, if I say, "Please pass me the ketchup," the fact that I experience ketchup differently than the other person, due to my particular taste buds and my "ketchup history", does not affect the successful passing of the ketchup. It is when we want to be understood in our unique, inner nature and experience, that language fails. It seems that the Rav identifies Adam the second as the one who requires this deeper communication to address a deep sense of loneliness. Adam the first just wants to get things done and language is quite adequate for this goal. The deeper communication is only possible among the Adam the second members within the Covenantal Community. The Rav states:

I mentioned previously that only the Covenantal Community consisting of all three grammatical *personae*- I, thou, and He-can and does alleviate the passional experience of Adam the second by offering him the opportunity to communicate, indeed to commune with, and to enjoy the genuine friendship of Eve. (LMOF, p. 53)

The Rav explains how this deeper communication takes place:

The change from a technical utilitarian relationship to a covenantal existential one occurs in the following manner. When God joins the community of man the miracle of revelation takes place in two dimensions: in the transcendental - *Deus absconditus* emerges suddenly as *Deus revelatus* - and in the human- *homo absconditus* sheds his mask and turns into *homo revelatus*. With the sound of the divine voice addressing man by his name, be it Abraham, Moses, or Samuel, God, whom man has sought all along the endless trails of the universe, is discovered suddenly as being close to and intimate with man, standing just opposite or beside him. At this meeting- initiated by God- of God and man, the covenantal-prophetic community is established. When man addresses himself to God, calling Him in the informal, friendly tones of "Thou" the same miracle happens again: God joins man and at this meeting, initiated by man, a new Covenantal Community is born- the prayer community. (LMOF, pp. 53-54)

So with the revelation of prophecy and the act of prayer we have the transformation of the relationship between man and God from one of separation and searching to one of a close and personal nature. In the revelation of prophecy and the Torah, God speaks to man in a personal way- not as the Creator and Master of the universe, but as a guide, a teacher and community builder. This relationship is continued when man stands in prayer and receives a personal audience with God in which man can petition and express his deepest inner feeling, knowing that they are fully comprehended by his maker. As the Rav states:

Prayer is basically an awareness of man finding himself in the presence of and addressing himself to his Maker, and to pray has one connotation only: to stand before God. (p. 56)

But how then does the personal relationship with God address the "communication gap" between people? What does the Covenantal Community contribute to resolving this issue? The Rav explains:

If God had not joined the community of Adam and Eve, they would have never been able and would have never cared to make the paradoxical leap over the gap, indeed abyss, separating two individuals whose personal experiential messages are written in a private code undecipherable by anyone else. Without the covenantal experience of the prophetic or prayerful colloquy, Adam *absconditus* would have persisted in his he-role and Eve *absconditus* in her she-role, unknown to and distant from each other. Only when God emerged from the transcendent darkness of He-anonymity into the illumined spaces of community knowability and charged man with an ethical and moral mission, did Adam absconditus and Eve abscondita, while revealing themselves to God in prayer and in unqualified commitment, also reveal themselves to each other in sympathy and love on the one hand and in common action on the other. Thus, the final objective of the human quest for redemption was attained; the individual felt relieved from loneliness and isolation. The community of the committed became, ipso facto, a community of friends - not of neighbors or acquaintances. Friendship-not as a social surface-relation but as an existential in-depth relation between two individuals-is realizable only within the framework of the Covenantal Community, where in-depth personalities relate themselves to each other ontologically and total commitment to God and fellow man is the order of the day. In the majestic community, in which surface personalities meet and commitment never exceeds the bounds of the utilitarian, we may find collegiality, neighborliness, civility, or courtesy-but not friendship, which is the exclusive experience awarded by God to covenantal man, who is thus redeemed from his agonizing solitude. (LMOF, pp. 68-69)

The Rav's explanation here of the relationship of Adam the second in the Covenantal Community is a pivotal part of the essay. This states how Adam the second's participation in the Covenantal Community relieves, to some degree, the loneliness that resulted from his cathartic redemptive experience and his realization of his incommunicable uniqueness and inherent loneliness. But the Rav's explanation here is quite brief and poetic and requires significant reflection and analysis on our part to understand its meaning.

The Rav makes clear that if it were not for God's revealing of Himself to man through the covenant, Adam would never have cared or considered to attempt to communicate with Eve (or any other person) in more than the surface practical manner of Adam the first. The inner self would remain hidden and unknown. ("If God had not joined…".) But when God reveals Himself in the covenant and "charged man with an ethical and moral mission"….this created an opening for man in two ways: 1) he was now able to have a close, personal relationship with God and 2) to structure all the activities of his life as an expression of that relationship.

I believe this idea can be understood in the following way:

1) Revelation and the covenant with its laws and directives, gave man the opportunity to transform the inner experience of redemption into a day to day life with activities and goals that form a communal life.

2) Adam the second and Eve, or any member of the Covenantal Community are now able to "also reveal themselves to each other in sympathy and love on the one hand and in common action on the other." The opportunity for true in-depth friendship now exists - "where in-depth personalities relate themselves to each other ontologically and total commitment to God and fellow man is the order of the day."

For a person to enter into a covenant with God requires the "activation" of the individual's deeper self, which is fundamentally bound to God. He is now able to act in the human community in a manner that stems from this commitment to the Covenant and his love of God, as opposed to being driven solely by the desire for mastery over his environment. The fulfillment of the Covenant does not make use of another person for selfish, pragmatic purposes, which is the structure of relationships between people in the Adam the first Work Community. Once an individual has been redeemed and realizes the true unique nature of each person, he no longer views others in a solely competitive or utilitarian manner, but as a co-struggler with this inner uniqueness and solitude and a partner in the activity of highest human value- the fulfillment of the Covenant.

This response is due to a recognition of one's own unique nature and a greater valuing of oneself and of every other individual. The Covenant allows for more than simply this recognition and sympathy. The Covenant requires of Adam the second that he dedicates his core being to acting on this recognition through the fulfillment of this Covenant. He understands that the fulfillment of the Covenant is not accomplished by the individual, but only by the community. Therefore, each person who partakes of the Covenantal Community is cherished by the others as they strive in communal action to fulfill the Covenant and serve their Creator. In contrast to the Adam the first Work Community paradigm, the other person in the Covenantal Community is not "used" by another to accomplish one's individual covenantal obligations. Together, as a community, members fulfill the Covenant's obligations. Also I believe that at the core of the Covenant is this valuing of each individual's unique nature.

Only together, in close connection, can redeemed men and women fulfill the greatest longing of their deepest inner self. In performing the obligations and requirements of the Covenant together (the only way they can be fulfilled) each person is bound to the others from the deepest self and recognizes and loves the most precious aspect of the other person. This is love and friendship in the deeper sense. When the Rav states, "personalities relate themselves to each other ontologically" he is explaining that this bond comes from the sharing of a common inner commitment and desire to fulfill their deepest human longing through their carrying out of the Covenant. The loneliness of Adam the second is not completely removed by this new connection. Each person's uniqueness still makes it impossible to express him or herself fully to others. However the loneliness is addressed and, to some extent, relieved. Perhaps we can clarify this incomplete, though fulfilling, connection through a parallel with God revealing Himself to people through the Covenant. God did not reveal to us His essence, but instead, His will and His requirements of us. But it is through this revelation that the member of the Covenantal Community are able to join with Him in love and community. So too, Adam the second is unable to reveal his unique essence to others, but through the "doing of the Covenant" and living by its directives, people join together to express their deepest inner longing for God. They too are "revealed" to each other as they endeavor to fulfill the longing of their most essential self. Although I cannot express to you my uniqueness and neither can you express yours to me, through the cooperative communal action of fulfilling the Covenant, we work together from each of our hidden inner selves to fulfill our deepest self's desire. The Rav stated earlier in the essay the complex amalgam of connection and separation of the members of the Covenantal Community:

Only when God emerged from the transcendent darkness of He-anonymity into the illumined spaces of community knowability and charged man with an ethical and moral mission, did Adam *absconditus* and Eve *absconditus*, while revealing themselves to God in prayer and in unqualified commitment, also reveal themselves to each other in sympathy and love on the one hand and in common action on the other. Thus, the final objective of the human quest for redemption was attained; the individual felt relieved from loneliness and isolation." (LMOF, p. 68)

The Covenantal Community's Past, Present & Future

The Rav describes the different views of time and finite existence that are experienced by Adam the first and Adam the second. Adam the first views time from a pragmatic, work point of view and is therefore not particularly troubled by his finite nature and its implications for his worth and value. Time is a factor in accomplishing tasks and is calculated in those terms. The Rav states:

Majestic man is not confronted with this time dilemma. The time with which he works and which he knows is quantified, spatialized, and measured, belonging to a cosmic coordinate system. Past and future are not two experiential realities. They just represent two horizontal directions. "Before" and "after" are understandable only within the framework of the causal sequence of events. (LMOF, p. 70)

Adam the second, on the other hand, whose quest is for redemption and is focused on the meaning and value of his existence and his part in the Creation, is greatly troubled by his temporary nature. He is confronted with the sense of his insignificance and his seemingly momentary existence. This situation conflicts with his quest for existential worthiness. How can a being that exists for a moment on the stream of time have any meaning or worth? The Rav states:

> The existential insecurity of Adam the second stems, to a great extent, also from his tragic role as a temporal being. He simply cannot pinpoint his position within the rushing stream of time. He knows of an endless past which rolled on without him. He is aware also of an endless future which will rush on with no less force long after he will cease to exist. The link between the "before" in which he was not involved and the "after" from which he will be excluded is the present moment, which vanishes before it is experienced. In fact, the whole accidental character of his being is tied up with this frightening time-consciousness. (LMOF, p. 69)

The Rav explains how Adam the second's participation in the Covenantal Community addresses and quells the tragic implications of man's temporary nature. By joining in the Covenantal Community in which God has revealed himself and has presented man with a united vision of history and man's place within it, from the first moment of Creation to culmination of man's journey in the time of the messiah, man becomes a meaningful participant in the full spectrum of history. His existence is no longer isolated within the brief moment of his physical life.

Every covenantal time experience is both retrospective, reconstructing and reliving the bygone, as well as prospective, anticipating the "about to be." In retrospect, covenantal man re-experiences the rendezvous with God in which the covenant, as a promise, hope, and vision, originated. In prospect, he beholds the full eschatological realization of this covenant, its promise, hope, and vision. (LMOF, p. 71)

The redeemed life of Adam the second, within the Covenantal Community's present fulfillment of the Divine will, has him, at the same time, "living in the past" as he personally accepts and experiences entering into the Covenant with God and "living in the future" as he envisions and endeavors to realize the future culmination of God's will on Earth in a post-messiah society. He experiences the past and the future of the Covenantal Community's events within his present, and they deeply inform his sense of the world and of himself. The Covenantal man of today doesn't simply read or study the past's history and envision the promised future. He experiences within himself, the leaving of Egypt, the gathering at Sinai, the glory of the building of the Temple and the mourning of its destruction. These events belong to him as much as to the people who experienced it in their actual present.

The Rav continues to explain, along these lines, that the Covenantal Community, which rests on the participation of God within the community, is beyond the time boundaries of past, present and future. The Covenantal Community is an eternal one, in which the past, present and future participants all join within one unified unfolding of a destiny that shares the timelessness of its most illustrious Member. The Rav states:

> Let us not forget that the Covenantal Community includes the "He" who addresses Himself to man not only from the "now" dimension but also from the supposedly already diminished past, from the ashes of a dead "before" facticity as well as from the as yet unborn future, for all boundaries establishing "before", "now", and "after" disappear when God the Eternal speaks. Within the Covenantal Community not only contemporary individuals but generations are engaged in a colloquy and each single experience of time is three-dimensional, manifesting itself in memory, actuality, and anticipatory tension. (LMOF, p. 71)

The Rav specifically addresses the Covenantal Community of the Jewish people. Even though the essay, up to this point, is supported with quotes and footnotes from the Talmud, Rashi, Maimonides, Nachmanides and other Jewish sources, the Covenantal Community, I would suggest, is not presented as a uniquely Jewish phenomenon. Although the essay does not touch on Noah and the covenant made between God and Noah after the flood, or on any other non-Jewish covenants, it does seem that all that has been described about Adam the first, Adam the second and the Covenantal Community applies to all who participate in these and other non-Jewish covenants with God. It is only here, three quarters of the way through the essay, where the focus is placed on the past, present and future joining together in the life of covenantal man, that the Rav describes the Jewish Covenantal Community and its characteristics. He states:

> The best illustration of such a paradoxical time awareness, which involves the individual in the historic performances of the past and makes him also participate in the dramatic action of an unknown future, can be found in the Judaic *masorah* community. The latter represents not only a formal succession within the framework of calendric time but the union of the three grammatical tenses in an all-embracing time experience. The *masorah* community cuts across the centuries, indeed millennia, of calendric time and unites those who already played their part, delivered their message, acquired fame, and withdrew from the covenantal stage quietly and humbly with those who have yet been given the opportunity to appear on the covenantal stage and who wait for their turn in the anonymity of the "about to be". (LMOF, pp. 71-72)

In this section of the essay, the Rav returns to the central role of prayer in its role of bringing man into the experiencing of past and future, within the present. He explains that when man communicates with God in prayer and God listens and receives his prayer, man experiences the connection to the Eternal One as well as the eternal community. It is through this bond that man's existential torment is relieved and by which he is redeemed. It is also by virtue of this joining that man takes on the awesome burden of covenantal responsibility- the fulfillment of man's role in upholding his "part of the bargain", his carrying out of the obligations and responsibilities of the Covenant. The Rav states of man:

He is no longer an evanescent being. He is rooted in everlasting time, in eternity itself. And so covenantal man confronts not only a transient contemporary "thou" but countless "thou" generations which advance toward him from all sides and engage him in the great colloquy in which God Himself participates with love and joy. This act of revelation does not avail itself of universal speech, objective logical symbols, or metaphors. The message communicated from Adam to Eve certainly consists of words. However, words do not always have to be identified with sound. It is rather a soundless revelation accomplished in muteness and in the stillness of the Covenantal Community. God responds to the prayerful outcry of lonely man and agrees to meet him as brother and friend, while man, in turn, assumes the great burden which is the price he pays for his encounter with God. (LMOF, p.73)

Although, the Rav does not discuss the experience of studying Torah in this essay, he has stated elsewhere how this core activity of the Jewish covenantal individual is a colloquy (an in-depth communication) with the scholars of the past and present. When the Rav discussed his own study of the great Jewish scholars of the past such as Rashi and the Rambam, he does not describe it as simply the reading of or understanding of the thoughts of another individual. The exhilarating experience resembled more of an ongoing continuing dialogue and intellectual battle that was alive, vital and deeply felt. The Rav argues with, agrees or disagrees with these great scholars, as if they were fully present within the study hall. This is a powerful example of the blending of past and present into one vibrant, living time-space.

Chapter 7
The Duality of Human Existence

Adam the second has found relief and redemption for his loneliness within the Covenantal Community. He has, to the extent possible, addressed the problem of his incommunicable uniqueness. The Rav states:

> The man of faith, as we explained previously, is lonely because of his being himself exclusively and not having a comrade, a "duplicate I." The man of faith, we further brought out, finds redemption in the covenantal faith community by dovetailing his accidental existence with the necessary existence of the Great True Self. There, we pointed out, *homo absconditus* turns into *homo relevatus* vis. a vis. God and man as well. (LMOF, p. 79)

It is true that the redemptive experience is a resolution of man's loneliness and his being confronted with the temporary nature of his existence. However, this solution is not a complete one. Man still consists of a dual nature that has him oscillating between the redemptive persona of Adam the second in his covenantal world and his majestic self as Adam the first in the Work Community. At one moment man is "home with God" within the existential continuity of the Covenantal Community and in the next moment he is isolated and alone as he switches to the role of majestic man within the natural, Work Community. The Rav states:

The man of faith, in his continuous movement between the pole of natural majesty and that of covenantal humility, is prevented from totally immersing in the immediate covenantal awareness of the redeeming presence, knowability, and involvement of God, in the community of man. From time to time the man of faith is thrown in the majestic community where the colloquy as well as the covenantal consciousness are swept away. (LMOF, p. 80)

The Rav, restates one of his central themes of the essay-that the majestic and the redemptive existence are both blessed. He makes clear that, unlike many pietistic co-religionists who place true value only on the redemptive experience, viewing any separation from one's immediate, personal connection to God as tragic, the Rav views the intent of the Creator to be that man's existence should also include the majestic dimension in which this separation must occur. This embracing of man's dual nature is a bold and illuminating insight by Rabbi Soloveitchik clarifying the meaning and structure of human life. Not only has the Rav brought the conquering, majestic element of man under the umbrella of serving God, but he has dispelled the misconception that the cloistered, meditative, passive existence of the classic "holy man" of any religion, be it Jewish, Christian, Moslem, Hindu, etc. is the true legitimate path for a man of God. To embrace the redemptive experience without the majestic is a violation of the will of the Creator and the nature of man, just as much as a rejection of the redemptive experience would be. As the Rav states:

He summoned man to retreat from peripheral, hard-won positions of vantage and power to the center of the faith experience. He also commanded man to advance from the covenantal center to the cosmic periphery and recapture the positions he gave up a while ago. He authorized man to quest for "sovereignty"; He also told man to surrender and be totally committed. (LMOF, p. 81)

The commandments of God enjoin man to walk down both of these two opposing paths in the fulfillment of his obligations to God. The Rav states:

On the one hand, the Bible commands man, "And thou shalt love the Lord thy God with all thy heart and with all thy soul and with all thy might," a performance of which only covenantal man is capable since he alone possesses the talent for complete concentration upon the immersion in the focus without being distracted by peripheral interests, anxieties, and problems. On the other hand, the same Bible which just enjoined man to withdraw from the periphery to the center commands him to return to the majestic community which, preoccupied with peripheral interests, anxieties, and problems, builds, plants, harvests, regulates rivers, heals the sick, participates in state affairs, is imaginative in dreaming, bold in planning, daring in undertaking and is out to "conquer" the world. (LMOF, pp. 81-82)

The Halakhah (Jewish Law) Reflects Man's Dual Nature

The Rav now describes how the halakhic system (Jewish law), which provides a path for human life, reflects these two parts of man – the redemptive and the majestic. The Rav goes so far as to suggest that the halakhah propels the person's movement between these two poles of his nature. The Rav states:

If one would inquire of me about the teleology of the Halakhah, I would tell him that it manifests itself exactly in the paradoxical yet magnificent dialectic which underlies of Halakhic gesture. When man gives himself to the Covenantal Community the Halakhah reminds him that he is also wanted and needed in another community, the cosmic-majestic, and when it comes across man while he is involved in the creative enterprise of the majestic community, it does not let him forget that he is a covenantal being who will never find self-fulfillment outside of the covenant and that God awaits his return to the Covenantal Community. (LMOF, pp. 82-83)

The Rav is describing how a person who is living the redemptive life and lives by the Torah's laws, will learn through this process, of his absolute responsibility to halt his redemptive involvements at some point, and return for a time to the responsibilities of majestic man in order to raise his family in a dignified and comfortable manner, build hospitals to help the sick, as well as build businesses and organizations to provide for the full spectrum of human needs. Similarly, the majestic man who involves himself in these projects and activities will be compelled by his inner sense that these accomplishments do not bring the feeling of fulfillment and completion that he searches for, to return to the covenantal life and its quest to address the deeper questions and the need for true companionship with God and man. The movement between these two poles continues unendingly. This is the life of man. Two currents running within the soul, each with its specific means of fulfillment. Unity of self and unity of purpose, however, are not achieved or even achievable. There always remains an element of despair and conflict in the human existence of the dual self.

Moses and the Patriarchs – The Merging of the Redemptive and Majestic Man

The Rav sees the full fruition of mankind to be the eventual merging of the majestic and redemptive spheres of existence into one. This is the fulfillment man will experience in the time of the Messiah. The Rav states:

Jewish eschatology beholds the great vision of a united majestic-Covenantal Community in which all oppositions will be reconciled and absolute harmony will prevail. When Zechariah proclaimed "the Lord shall be King over all the earth; on that day the Lord shall be one and His name one," he referred not to the unity of God, which is absolute and perfect even now, but to the future unity of creation, which is currently torn asunder by inner contradictions. On that distant day the dialectical process will come to a close and man of faith as well as majestic man will achieve full redemption in a united world. (LMOF, p. 87)

To help us understand and envision this unified man that will emerge on a global scale at the time of the Messiah, the Rav focuses on Moses and the Patriarchs as mankind's only individuals to have achieved the unification of the redemptive and majestic personae into one unified whole. The Rav states:

Maimonides distinguishes between two kinds of dialectic: (1) the constant oscillating between the majestic and the Covenantal Community; (2) the simultaneous involvement in both communities, which is the higher form of dialectical existence and which, according to Maimonides, only Moses and the Patriarchs achieved." (LMOF, p. 88)

The Rav quotes Maimonides' Mishnah Torah (Foundations of the Torah 8:6) where this unique unification of the redemptive and the majestic is described in the life of Moses. The Rambam states:

Hence it may be inferred that all prophets when the prophetic power left them returned to their tents, that they attended to the satisfaction of their physical needs. Moses, our teacher, never went back to his former tent. He, accordingly, permanently separated himself from his wife, and abstained from similar gratifications. His mind was closely attached to the Rock of the Universe. (LMOF, p. 88)

The Rav explains how Moses, though he never left the covenantal mode, was, however, simultaneously involved in the fulfillment of the majestic, Adam the first, agenda. The Rav states:

This, however, is not to be interpreted as if Moses had abandoned the majestic community. After all, Moses dedicated his life to the fashioning of a majestic-Covenantal Community bent on conquest and political-economic normalcy on the one hand, and the realization of the covenantal kerygma on the other. (LMOF, p. 88)

Though Moses never left the presence of God to "return" to Adam the first's world of majesty, with its focus on man's dominion over nature and the pursuit of dignity, he did pursue the mission of "subduing the world" to the word of God. In this highest level of human existence, it seems, even acts of conquest and dominance are contained within the person's experiencing of God's presence - within his experiencing of the redemption of God. The Rav then quotes the Rambam's "Guide for the Perplexed" which describes how the Patriarchs also maintained a continuous covenantal connection to God while, at the same time, fulfilling the needs of man's majestic calling to transform the world according to God's will. The Rav quotes Rambam's "Guide for the Perplexed" at this point, stating:

The Patriarchs likewise attained this degree of perfection....When we therefore find them also engaged in ruling others, in increasing their property and endeavoring to obtain possession of wealth and honor, we see in this fact a proof that when they were occupied in in these things their bodily limbs were at work while their heart and mind never moved away from the name of God. (LMOF, p. 88)

It seems to me that the Rambam, as understood by the Rav, is not describing a homogenous, equal blending of the redemptive and covenantal man into a united whole. The character of Moses and the Patriarchs were solely covenantal. They never departed from the direct presence of God. However, unlike the "normal" redemptive man who, when in the redemptive, covenantal mode, is motivated to a mindset of passive submission and obedience, Moses and the Patriarchs were capable of channeling their drive to "be fruitful and multiply and conquer the earth and subdue it" in order to operate fully within the covenantal domain. Their acts of conquest and dominion were not, as with the typical Adam the first, a selfish drive connected to the desire for mastery and dignity, but instead were simply another element in their ongoing and direct relationship with God. This is a level only achieved by the highest of our prophets. The rest of us must wait for the Messianic age for this unity of self.

The Majestic Character of the Halakhah

The Rav continues his description of the legitimacy of the majestic (Adam the first) character living in tandem with covenantal man by making a strong statement regarding the majestic dimension of the Jewish covenant – the system of Jewish law also known as the "halakhah". The commandments, which define the boundaries of covenantal man's life and are his means of cleaving to his Creator and living the redeemed life, are themselves, replete with majestic character which encourages and commands humanity to conquer and transform the world of nature into a place of human dignity and human dominion The Rav states:

> The unqualified acceptance of the world of majesty by the Halakhah expresses itself in its natural and inevitable involvement in every sector of human majestic endeavor. There is not a single theoretical or technological discovery, from new psychological insights into the human personality to man's attempt to reach out among the planets, with which the Halakhah is not concerned. As a matter of fact, at present, in order to render precise Halakhic decisions in many fields of human endeavor, one must possess, besides excellent Halakhic training, a good working knowledge of those secular fields in which the problem occurs. (LMOF, pp. 88-89)

The Halakhic system's absolute dedication to healing and saving of the life of the sick and injured, the Rav explains, is a fundamental expression of the majestic character of Jewish law. He rejects completely and passionately a religious view that is based wholly on acceptance of fate and that lauds a passive approach to these "evils" as being "God's will". He states:

> This acceptance, easily proven in regard to the total majestic gesture, is most pronounced in the Halakhah's relationship to scientific medicine and the art of healing. The latter has always been considered by the Halakhah as a great and noble occupation. Unlike other faith communities, the Halakhic community has never been troubled by the problem of human interference, on the part of the physician and patient, with God's will. On the contrary, argues the Halakhah, God wants man to fight evil bravely and

to mobilize all his intellectual and technological ingenuity in order to defeat it. The conquest of disease is the sacred duty of man of majesty and he must not shirk it. (LMOF, p. 89)

The Rav goes on to dispel any misconception that the concept of "betuchan" or "faith" in God's kindness carries with it a totally passive approach to confronting pain, disease and other destructive elements within a person's life. This misunderstanding of God 's expectation of mankind fails on two counts: 1- it denies the majestic element within man's basic character and the innate drive towards accomplishment, creativity and dignity which is fundamental to his soul. 2- it denies the blessing God has given to man to "be fruitful and multiply and have dominion over the Earth". The Rav states:

The doctrine of faith in God's charity, "betuchan", is not to be equated with the folly of the mystical doctrine of quietism, which in its extreme form exempts man from his duty of attending to his own needs and lets him wait in "holy" idleness and indifference for God's intervention. This kind of repose is wholly contrary to the repose which the Halakhah recommends: the one which follows human effort and remedial action. Man must first use his own skill and try to help himself as much as possible. Then, and only then, man may find repose and quietude in God and be confident that his effort and action will be crowned with success. LMOF, p. 90)

Chapter 8
The Contemporary Dismissal of Adam the Second and the Redemptive Life

The Rav assesses modern man to be totally enamored with the majestic, dignified dimension of life and totally dismissive of the redemptive one. The Rav is careful to point out that this trend is not found only in the atheist or the irreligious person, but in religious community members as well. Being part of the religious community does not, in itself, actualize a person's redemptive persona. Religious life and its pursuits can become completely subsumed in the pursuit of dignity and majesty, with no involvement in the redemptive, covenantal experience. The Rav explains:

Let me diagnose the situation in a few terse sentences. Contemporary Adam the first, extremely successful in his cosmic-majestic enterprise, refuses to pay earnest heed to the duality in man and tries to deny the undeniable, that another Adam exists beside or, rather, in him. By rejecting Adam the second, contemporary man, *eo ipso*, dismisses the covenantal faith community as something superfluous and obsolete. To clear up any misunderstanding on the part of my audience, I wish to note that I am not concerned in this essay with the vulgar and illiterate atheism professed and propagated in the most ugly fashion by a natural-political community which denies the unique transcendental worth of the human personality, I am referring rather to Western man who is affiliated with organized religion and is a generous supporter of its institutions. He stands today in danger of losing his dialectical awareness and of abandoning completely the metaphysical polarity implanted in man as a member of both the majestic and the Covenantal Community. (LMOF, p. 92)

Modern man has made such unprecedented strides in the area of technology and mastery over the environment during the past 200 years, that it has distorted his view of the nature of human existence. This mastery over nature, achieved through the breathtaking successes of technology and scientific method, has given rise to unimagined gains in controlling disease and extending the lifespan as well as improvements in architecture, transportation, and communications. These achievements have resulted in a tremendous improvement in man's general level of convenience and his level mastery over the external environment. These accomplishments align with the goals of Adam the first's quest for dominion and are a fulfillment of God's blessing to man, "be fruitful and multiply and conquer the earth". But it is the overwhelming nature of this progress, according to the Rav, that has led to a disturbance of the balance between Adam the first and Adam the second. The redemptive life, by which man quests for his essential nature by his being recognized by his Creator and through his unqualified service to God, has been all but swept away by the power of the majestic accomplishments of contemporary Adam the first.

The Rav explains how this shift impacts the religious community as well. Religion, like other human cultural endeavors, can be subsumed under the agenda of Adam the first. When religion and religious life becomes solely a means for achieving a dignified, orderly and civilized way of living, it is transformed into an Adam the first activity. Externally, the religious community may appear covenantal, as it carries out the laws and customs of God's commandments. But the nature of the community is determined by its inner drives and interests. If religious life is utilized by a person as just another element of his living a civilized, efficient lifestyle, it must be considered solely majestic and not redemptive. In this case, God does not have a personal, active role in the religious community. God may be its inspiration, but He is not a participant in its life. The Rav compares the covenantal and the religious communities:

The two communities are as far apart as the two Adams. While the covenantal faith community is governed, as I emphasized, by a desire for a redeemed existence, the religious community is dedicated to the attainment of dignity and success and is – along with the whole gamut of communities such as the political, the scientific, the artistic- a creation of Adam the first, all conforming to the same sociological structural patterns. The religious community is, therefore, also a Work Community consisting of two grammatical *personae* not including the Third Person. The prime purpose is the successful furtherance of the interests, not the deepening and enhancing of the commitments, of man who values religion in terms of its usefulness to him and considers the religious act a medium through which he may increase his happiness. (LMOF, pp. 92-93)

The Rav does not disdain the idea that religious life has a legitimate role in the achieving of dignity by Adam the first. As we discussed at length, the majestic life also seeks to carry out the will of God and to fulfill the blessing of "be fruitful and multiply" given to man by his Creator. Majestic man's civilization would be incomplete and unsatisfying without the moral and existential legitimacy given to it by being a fulfillment of the divine command to build a world. Once again, it is not the fulfillment of the majestic which is the error here. The mistake is conceiving of the majestic dimension as encompassing the entirely of human life and man's sole destiny. The Rav explains:

This assumption on the part of majestic man about the role of religion is not completely wrong, if only, as I shall explain, he would recognize also the non-pragmatic aspects of religion. Faith is indeed relevant to man not only metaphysically, but also practically. It gives his life, even at the secular mundane level, a new existential dimension. (LMOF, p. 93)

The Rav then explains a key point - that Adam the first's majestic strivings are not independent of Adam the second's redemptive path. The majestic goals of Adam the first requires the redemptive efforts of Adam the second in order to succeed. There is a symbiosis and mutual dependency here.

It is very certain and self-evident that Adam the first cannot succeed completely in his efforts to attain majesty-dignity without having the man of faith contribute his share. The cultural edifice whose great architect Adam the first is would be built on shifting sands if he sought to conceal from

himself and from others the fact that he alone cannot implement the mandate of majesty-dignity entrusted to him by God and that he must petition Adam the second for help. (LMOF, pp. 93-94)

What is the help that Adam the second provides to assist Adam the first in his quest for majesty? He is not really required for the physical aspects of Adam the first's work. Cities and bridges can be built. Technology can progress. Scientific breakthroughs and medical advances have no need of Adam the second's redeemed life. But, perhaps something even more fundamental to the basic striving of Adam the first for mastery is the deep desire to understand "what is true?", "what is beautiful?" and "what is real?". These interests are deeply imbedded in the pursuits of majestic man. The Rav states:

He is questing not only for material success, but for the ideological and axiological achievements as well. He is concerned with a philosophy of nature and man, of matter and mind, of things and ideas. Adam the first is not only a creative mind, incessantly looking and pressing forward, but also a mediating mind, casting a backward glance and appraising his handiwork, thereby imitating his Maker who, at the end of each stage of creation, inspected and appraised it. Adam frequently interrupts his forward march, turns around, views and evaluates his creative accomplishments, making an effort to place them in some philosophical and axiological perspective. (LMOF, pp. 94-95)

But, the Rav explains that without an understanding and experiencing of the redemptive life, majestic man will make no meaningful progress in the clarification of these key areas.

For the retrospective appraisal and appreciation of the cognitive drama as well as the successful performance at the ethico-moral and aesthetic levels are unattainable as long as man moves continuously within the closed, vicious cycle of the insensate natural occurrence and never reaches "beyond". (LMOF, p. 95)

In addition, Adam the first's entire edifice of civilization rests on the validity of an ethical/moral system. Adam the first's technology and power can allow him to accomplish great feats, but it does not really inform him of moral truths or what constitutes "the good". He can accomplish things efficiently and quickly, but the question remains "what activities are worthy of being accomplished?". Only the moral/ethical sphere can give meaning to the majestic. Without this, Adam the first is unable to sustain a civilization, as it does not address man's basic need to satisfy his sense of himself as a moral being pursuing the good. The well-spring of this ethical/moral system is the covenant of Adam the second. This covenant gives morality the quality of reality as its source is from the True Real Self. Without this to build on, Adam the first builds "on shifting sand".

In a like manner, the worth and validity of the ethical norm, if it is born of the finite creative-social gesture of Adam the first, cannot be upheld. Only

the sanctioning by a higher moral will is capable of lending to the norm fixity, permanence, and worth. (LMOF, p. 96)

The aesthetic sphere, so central to the majestic man's plan for creating a civilization that reflects his stature and vision, with its pursuit of beauty in art, music, architecture, writing and other mediums, is hollow without the redemptive dimension. The aesthetic, it seems, draws its core force from the redemptive as well. Man's encounter with God, which is the core of the redemptive experience, is the source of the impulse to create beauty as well. The Rav states:

In a similar fashion, the aesthetic experience to which contemporary man abandons himself with almost mystical ecstasy remains incomplete as long as beauty does not rise to sublimity and remains unredeemed. However, redemption is a covenantal category and the sublime is inseparable from the exalted. And how can majestic man be confronted with redeemed beauty in which the exalted is reflected if he is enclosed in a dreary mechanical world from which he has neither strength nor courage to free himself. In short, the message of faith, if translated into cultural categories, fits into the axiological and philosophical frame of reference of the creative cultural consciousness and is pertinent even to secular man. (LMOF, p. 96)

The Crisis in Relations Between Majestic and Redemptive Man

The contemporary man of faith (i.e. Adam the second/redemptive man) and majestic man are not in communication with each other. Contemporary majestic man fails to see the importance of the redemptive experience and has not sought out redemptive man's unique insight in his "conquest of the world". Redemptive man has been unable to translate the redemptive experience into terms that can be understood and utilized by majestic man. This tragic state of affairs has resulted in fundamentally hindering the accomplishments of majestic man, as the Rav has clarified up to this point. It has also resulted in the man of faith being marginalized and "dismissed" as far as his role in contributing to human civilization. The Rav envisions the satisfaction that the man of faith would experience if this situation were resolved:

> If the job of translating faith mysteries into cultural aspects could be fully accomplished, then contemporary man of faith could free himself, if not from the ontological awareness which is perennial, then, at least, from the peculiar feeling of psychological loneliness and anguish which is due to his historical confrontation with the man of culture. The man of faith would, if this illusion came true, be at peace with the man of culture so that the latter would fully understand the significance of human dialectics, and a perfect harmonious relationship would prevail between both Adams. (LMOF, p. 98)

The Rav makes clear that this "harmonious relationship" can never fully be realized. There is an existential problem that prevents it. Adam the first views the world through the process and categories of logic. Only knowledge derived through this method is viewed as valid and it is all that he can understand. It is the logical categories of the mind and their application that are the source of Adam the first's power. These are the tools with which he has built his world and how he understands it. The redemptive experience of Adam the second does not translate into logical categories. The Rav states:

> However, this harmony can never be attained since the man of faith is not the compromising type and his covenantal commitment eludes cognitive analysis by the *logos* and hence does not lend itself completely to the act of cultural translation. There are simply no cognitive categories in which the total commitment of the man of faith could be spelled out. (LMOF, p. 99)

The primal encounter with one's true, real, self and its impact on one's perspective and sense of reality cannot be fully expressed in a logical form. The experience is one that occurs on multiple levels of the personality and its transformative effects are experienced as profound but are not translatable into specific words and sentences and even less so into a linear, logical presentation. The Rav states:

> The whole of the human being, the rational as well as the non-rational aspects, is committed to God. Hence the magnitude of the commitment is beyond the comprehension of the *logos* and the *ethos*. The act of faith is aboriginal, exploding with elemental force as an all-consuming and all-pervading, eudaemonic-passional experience in which our most secret urges, aspirations, fears and passions, at times even unsuspected by us, manifest themselves. The commitment of the man of faith is thrown into the mold of the in-depth personality and immediately accepted before the mind is given a chance to investigate the reasonableness of this unqualified commitment. (LMOF, pp. 99-100)

The Rav describes briefly the unique cognitive process of majestic man and redemptive man. Majestic man (aka-Adam the first) is a man of logic and a master of its application. It defines his view of truth. The redemptive man of faith is also an intellect who brings reason and logic to bear. But in the case of redemptive man, logic does not discover truth, it describes it. The redemptive experience, it seems, "comes upon him" through his inherent, aboriginal connection to God. He experiences this connection by virtue of his very essence. He does not arrive at it by "figuring it out" or solving a series of problems. However, he does bring all of his cognitive skills to bear in order to describe it in words and expressions that capture, imperfectly, the qualities of his experience. The Rav explains:

The intellect does not chart the course of the man of faith; its role is an *a posteriori* one. It attempts, *ex post facto,* to retrace the footsteps of the man of faith, and even in this modest attempt the intellect is not completely successful. (LMOF, p. 100)

There is an overlap between logic and faith. But a point is reached where logic cannot account for or describe the covenantal experience. At this point reason and faith part ways. The Rav states:

The man of faith animated by his great experience is able to reach the point at which not only his logic of the mind but even his logic of the heart and of the will, everything-even his own "I" awareness-has to give in to an "absurd" commitment. The man of faith is "insanely" committed to and "madly" in love with God. (p. 100)

The Rav, interestingly, quotes Maimonides at this point, citing the Mishneh Torah-Laws of Repentance, where this experience of being "enraptured" and "lovesick" for God is described. Maimonides, the greatest of the Jewish rationalist, is brought as a paradigmatic example of the redemptive man (Adam the second)! One could speculate that the Rav's choice of the Rambam for this role is to show that the redemptive experience, though not fully assailable in logical terms, is at the core of the religious experience for even the most highly developed rationalist. Maimonides is quoted:

What is the love of God that is befitting? It is to love the Eternal with a great and exceeding love, so strong that one's soul shall be knit up with the love of God, and one should be continually enraptured by it, like a lovesick individual whose mind is at no time free from its passion. (LMOF, p. 100)

It is redemptive man - Adam the second, that experiences the love of God (*Ahavas Hashem*). This "lovesickness" and "rapture" should not be confused with the malady of those overcome by physical/emotional desire and passion for an individual. In the case of the romantic lover, this "lovesickness" results from a degeneration of the person who has allowed the bodily urges to take control of his mind and will. In the case of the love of God (*Ahavas Hashem*), although the experience may share the quality of being overwhelmed and fixated on the object of desire, in this case the love results from the deepest, most essential aspect of man soul- his attachment to his

Creator. The romantic is lost in an illusion where lust distorts his accurate assessment of the love object and he overestimates its worth. In the case of the "lovesick" lover of God, this is certainly not the case. The experience is due to a person's coming to realize in his limited way, the truly infinite value of God, which brings him to this state of overwhelming desire. This assessment is an accurate one and the result of a recognition of the most fundamental of truths. It does, however, result in a state of mind which is overwhelming in its desire and intensity of focus. The redemptive experience of Adam the second cannot be communicated in terms that Adam the first can fully grasp. There will be aspects of the redemptive experience that Adam the first will see as positive and beneficial, but he will be unable to relate to its essence. The Rav gives an example of this, regarding prayer:

Prayer, for instance, might appeal to majestic man as he most uplifting, integrating and purifying act, arousing the finest and noblest emotions, yet these characteristics, however essential to Adam the first, are of marginal interest to Adam the second, who experiences prayer as the awesome confrontation of God and man, as the great paradox of man conversing with God as an equal fellow member of the covenantal society, and at the same time being aware that he fully belongs to God and that God demands complete surrender and self-sacrifice. (LMOF, p. 101)

The chasm that exists between the perspectives of the redemptive man and majestic man must be accepted. Their collaboration is not one that results from simply finding common ground. On the contrary, Adam the first's way to "best make use" of Adam the second's unique and incomprehensible perspective begins with Adam the first accepting that the redemptive experience can never be understood in majestic terms or activities. The Rav states:

In a word, the message of translated religion is not the only one which the man of faith must address to majestic man of culture. Besides this message, man of faith must bring to the attention of man of culture the *kerygma* of the original faith in all its singularity and pristine purity, in spite of the incomprehensibility of this message with the fundamental credo of a utilitarian society. (LMOF, p. 102)

There does not seem to be a well-defined, specific role for redemptive man in the activities of majestic man. However redemptive man's participation is essential for the majestic man's world to prosper. Redemptive man's experience must be accepted as real and true by Adam the first, even though he cannot utilize it in a direct manner to help achieve his ends of conquest and control. To ignore the influence and meaningfulness of the direct encounter with God experienced by redemptive man and the Covenantal Community would undermine the purpose of Adam the first's accomplishments. It is this God/man encounter and the relationship that ensues, that is at the core of the human individual and community experience and which nourishes the deepest most fundamental core of the human personality. To dismiss this is to misunderstand what it means to be human and the ultimate purpose of human civilization. (This is not a minor error, to say the least.)

But redemptive man's message, which appears at first to stand diametrically opposed to that of majestic man is afforded no place or consideration in Adam the first's world of precision and power. The Rav describes Adam the first's logic and the tragic result of his inability to grant validity and place to redemptive man.

How staggering this incomprehensibility is! This unique message speaks of defeat instead of success, of accepting a higher will instead of commanding, of giving instead of conquering, of retreating instead of advancing, of acting "irrationally" instead of being always reasonable. Here the tragic event occurs. Contemporary majestic man rejects his dialectical assignment and with it, the man of faith. (LMOF, p. 102)

The Modern Marginalization of Redemptive Man

Toward the close of LMOF, the Rav returns to the discussion raised at the beginning of the essay. The unprecedented accomplishments of modern majestic man's science and technology with his breakthroughs in so many areas, have magnified his profile to such a level that it has left no discernible role for redemptive man. The Rav compares this contemporary delusion of grandeur to the episode of the Tower of Babel in Genesis. The Rav states:

The situation has deteriorated considerably in this century, which has witnessed the greatest triumphs of majestic man in his drive for conquest.

112

Majestic Adam has developed a demonic quality laying claim to unlimited power-alas to infinity itself. His pride is almost boundless, his imagination arrogant and he aspires to complete and absolute control of everything. Indeed like the men of old, he is engaged in constructing a tower whose apex should pierce Heaven. (LMOF, p. 102)

The amazing accomplishments of human creativity have brought us to mistakenly identify man's creative impulse with his full essence. This sense of power and exaltation that Adam the first experiences from his involvement in the creative process resists the subservient, humble stance of the redemptive man's communion with God. The Rav explains that even man's religious life, in the present day, does not embrace the sacrificial acts and unqualified commitment of redemptive man, but, instead seeks a peaceful and serene state of mind as his goal. This search for serenity is another element in majestic man's quest for mastery and control over his own life. The Rav states:

He, of course, comes to a place of worship. He attends lectures on religion and appreciates the ceremonial, yet he is searching not for a faith in all its singularity and otherness, but for a religious culture. He seeks not the greatness found in sacrificial action but the convenience one discovers in a comfortable, serene state of mind. (LMOF, p. 103)

What is Adam the first striving for through his religious experience? He is seeking success in ways that he cannot accomplish through other means. The Rav explains that he seeks to utilize religion as a means to experience beauty, to enhance his ethical structures and in feeling assured that he is a person who is truly blessed. These are extensions of Adam the first's majestic enterprise of mastery, control and dignity. These aspects of religion can be very useful in helping Adam the first complete his program. The Rav states:

He is desirous of an aesthetic experience rather than a covenantal one, of a social ethos rather than a divine imperative. In a word he wants to find in faith that which he cannot find in his laboratory, or in the privacy of his luxurious home. His efforts are noble, yet he is not ready for a genuine faith experience which requires the giving of oneself unreservedly to God, who demands unconditional commitment, sacrificial action and retreat. Western man diabolically insists on being successful even in his adventure with God. If he gives of himself to God, he expects reciprocity. He also reaches a covenant with God, but this covenant is a mercantile one. In a primitive manner he wants to trade "favors" and exchange goods. (LMOF, pp. 103-104)

Chapter 9

The Unchanging Character of the Faith Experience

The man of faith has a role in presenting aspects of the religious experience in the terminology and categories that are relevant to the culture of the time and place he finds himself. His ability to impact and shape the general culture will depend on these contemporary expressions. For example certain psychological categories or scientific categories may be utilized to clarify the positive aspects of the faith experience on the lives of people. But the Rav explains that the core experience by which God and man meet within the Covenantal Community and within the deep recesses of the soul's core, are not subject to the change and flux associated with contemporary culture. Man's unqualified commitment to God and the life that results from that commitment, are unchanged by the time and place where he find's himself. The faith experience is not an evolving, developing one. It is a gift given from the perfect, infinite God to imperfect, finite man. Man cannot alter or improve it. The Rav states:

Certainly, when the man of faith interprets his transcendental awareness in cultural categories, he takes advantage of modern interpretive methods and is selective in picking his categories. The cultural message of faith changes, indeed, constantly, with the flow of time, the shifting of the spiritual climate, the fluctuations of axiological moods, and the rise of social needs. However, the act of faith itself is unchangeable, for it transcends the bounds of time and space. Faith is born of the intrusion of eternity upon temporality. Its essence is characterized by fixity and enduring identity. Faith is experienced not as a product of some emergent evolutionary process, or as something which has been brought into existence by man's creative cultural gesture, but as something which was given to man when the latter was overpowered by God. Its prime goal is redemption from the inadequacies of finitude and mainly, from the flux of temporality. (LMOF, p. 105)

Modern man, who revels in the majestic, must come to realize that the man of faith can and must assist him in his quest for dignity and control. However, to be effective, the faith experience must remain unaltered and unaffected by time, place or culture. If the great redemptive experience of the man of faith is allowed to become a branch of human culture, shifting and changing with the times, it will lose its redemptive power and will also be of no significant use to Adam the first in establishing his majestic progress on firm ground.

He (Adam the first) fails to realize that the reality of the power of faith, which may set modern man free from anxiety and neurotic complexes and help him plan the strategy of invincible majestic living, can only be experienced if the faith gesture is left alone, outside of the fleeting stream of socio-cultural metamorphoses and tolerated as something stable and immutable. If the faith gesture should be cut loose from its own absolute moorings and allowed to float upon the mighty waters of historical change, then it will forfeit its redemptive and therapeutic qualities. (LMOF, p. 106)

In the face of an Adam the first who lacks understanding and who is unwilling to validate the act of faith, redemptive man withdraws from the greater society and remains separated and cut off from participating in the process of the developing contemporary culture.

It is here that the dialogue between the man of faith and the man of culture comes to an end. Modern Adam the second, as soon as he finishes translating religion into the cultural vernacular and begins to talk the "foreign" language of faith, finds himself lonely, forsaken, misunderstood, at times even ridiculed by Adam the first, by himself. When the hour of estrangement strikes, the ordeal of man of faith begins and he starts his withdrawal from society, from Adam the first-be he an outsider, be he himself. He returns, like Moses of old to his solitary hiding and to the abode of loneliness. (LMOF, p. 106)

The man of faith now experiences two "lonelinesses" - the existential loneliness of being unique and unable to communicate this uniqueness to any other equally unique person, and the additional loneliness of living in a society that does not validate or recognize his vital and fundamental faith experience nor values it in building the world. But the man of faith continues to attempt to break through and make the act of faith and covenantal understanding something that is embraced by majestic man as essential to his mission.

Chapter 10

Summary and Conclusion

The lonely man of faith which the Rav describes so beautifully in this
essay is also termed "Adam the second" and "redemptive man".
They are all one and the same. He is a person who has partaken of
the redemptive experience by which a person realizes his or her own
uniqueness and inherent value as a one-of-a-kind creation capable of
communing with God in a singular way. This communing is most
fundamentally experienced in prayer, but permeates the whole
existence of the redeemed individual. The experience of redemption
can only come to one who is defeated and overwhelmed by God and
stands in unconditional commitment and servitude to the One True
Being. This relationship does not degrade the redeemed person but
instead fills him or her with a sense of inherent worth that cannot be
diminished by poverty, sickness or even shame. Only sin, which is a
willful turning away from God, can assail this redemption and the
sense of one's "right to exist" that is experienced by the redeemed
person. Once redeemed and aware of his or her unique character, the
redeemed person is beset with a realization that he or she cannot be
truly understood by any other human being. Each one of us has a
unique essence that is not truly communicable in words or otherwise,
to any other human being. The Rav describes this "existential

loneliness" as being inherent to the redeemed person and not a result of his or her time, place or circumstance.

This loneliness of redeemed individuals receives some relief by their joining together in the Covenantal Community. Here, these lonely individuals, in complete unconditional dedication to God, join together to assist each other in this noble quest. In doing so, the members of the Covenantal Community join together in the deepest, most loving way possible for human beings. The members of this community, recognize each other's uniqueness, but also through knowing that they all have a common goal of fulfilling God's covenant, form a community in which they are joined not by selfish purposes related to power and mastery, but in the mutual actualization of their attachment to God. The Rav makes clear that God participates actively within this community, hearing prayer, responding to the needs of the community and letting His Wisdom and Will be known through the revelation of the covenant.

The essay clarifies the alter ego of the redeemed man – Adam the first, also known as majestic man. This dimension of the human personality is found in the dignified, problem solving conqueror of nature who builds a human civilization of beauty, intelligence and service to God. But Adam the first is concerned with the accomplishment of a dignified, orderly and stable life. Even majestic man's interest in religion is focused on these ends. Majestic man is in great ascendancy today with his unprecedented technological accomplishments and the success of scientific inquiry. This rise of Adam the first to such heights has greatly obscured and marginalized the importance and validity of Adam the second and the redemptive experience. The Rav explains how this has caused a second type of loneliness in the man of faith. He views himself as having no role in the building of contemporary human civilization. He is viewed as archaic, useless and no longer needed. This situation, the Rav describes, is not only detrimental to the state of the redeemed man, but is a fatal flaw in the majestic plan of Adam the first. Without the acceptance and understanding of the redemptive dimension of human life, Adam the first's majestic world is a fragile one, lacking true beauty, morality and meaning. It is only when Adam the first fully accepts, validates and confers with the great redemptive and covenantal experience of Adam the second that Adam the first will be able to build a civilization that has true majesty and beauty.

About the Author

Rabbi Richard Borah received smicha in 1991 from Rabbi Yisrael Chait, Rosh Yeshiva of Yeshiva Bnei Torah, located in Far Rockaway, New York. He has taught Torah and science subjects at various education institutions in the New York area. Rabbi Borah recently published " Yad on the Yad: 14 Essays on Maimonides Laws of Repentance". He has also recently completed a weekly series "the Rambam and the Rav on the Parsha" which compares the views of Maimonides and Rabbi Yoseph B. Soloveitchik's on issues from the weekly Torah reading. He hopes to publish these as a book in the near future. Rabbi Borah lives in Hewlett, New York with his wife Andrea and their children.

To receive weekly articles, purchase copies of books or for other inquires please send an email request to Rabbi Borah at: rambamrav@gmail.com.

Books are also available at amazon.com

Made in the USA
Lexington, KY
04 September 2013